THE END OF PUBLIC SCHOOLS

The End of Public Schools analyzes the effect of foundations, corporations, and non-governmental organizations on the rise of neoliberal principles in public education. By first contextualizing the privatization of education within the context of a larger educational crisis, and with particular emphasis on the Gates Foundation and influential state and national politicians, this book describes how specific policies that limit public control are advanced across all levels. Informed by a thorough understanding of issues such as standardized testing, teacher tenure, and charter schools, David W. Hursh provides a political and pedagogical critique of the current school reform movement, as well as details about the increasing resistance efforts on the part of parents, teachers, and the general public.

David W. Hursh is Professor of Teaching and Curriculum in the Graduate School of Education and Human Development at the University of Rochester, NY, USA.

The Critical Social Thought Series
Edited by Michael W. Apple
University of Wisconsin–Madison

THE END OF PUBLIC SCHOOLS

The Corporate Reform Agenda to Privatize Education

David W. Hursh

Routledge
Taylor & Francis Group

NEW YORK AND LONDON

First published 2016
by Routledge
711 Third Avenue, New York, NY 10017

and by Routledge
2 Park Square, Milton Park, Abingdon, Oxon, OX14 4RN

Routledge is an imprint of the Taylor & Francis Group, an informa business

Library of Congress Cataloging-in-Publication Data
Hursh, David W., 1948–
    The end of public schools : the corporate reform agenda to privatize
education / by David W. Hursh.
        pages cm. — (Critical social thought)
    Includes bibliographical references and index.
    1. Privatization in education.   2. Capitalism and
education.   3. Neoliberalism.   I. Title.
    LB2806.36.H87 2015
    379.1—dc23
    2015019624

ISBN: 978-1-138-80448-7 (hbk)
ISBN: 978-1-138-80449-4 (pbk)
ISBN: 978-1-315-75298-3 (ebk)

Typeset in Bembo
by Apex CoVantage, LLC

CONTENTS

SERIES EDITOR INTRODUCTION

Michael W. Apple

The first sentence of David Hursh's book jumps out at you: "We may be witnessing the end of public education in the United States." This statement demands our attention in a way that forces the reader to focus on a considerable number of forces that are challenging the very nature of our public school system and the policies and practices that underpin it.

Let me place this in its larger context, a context that *The End of Public Schools* critically analyses so well. In the United States, but not just here, dominant groups have increasingly focused on education as the source of a large portion of our society's problems. They have attempted, often more than a little successfully, to limit criticism, to control access to research that documents the negative effects of their policies, and to deny the possibility of critically democratic alternatives. They have pressed forward with an agenda in education—and in so much more— that is claimed to simply guarantee efficiency, effectiveness, and cost savings. For them, only these kinds of policies can deal with the crisis in education—even when they are demonstrably wrong.

These groups are not totally wrong in grounding their "reforms" in a sense of crisis. Across the political spectrum, it is widely recognized that there is a crisis in education. Nearly everyone agrees that something must be done to make it more responsive and more effective. Of course, a key set of questions is: responsive to what and to whom? Effective at what? And whose voices will be heard in asking and answering these questions? These are among the most crucial questions one can ask about education today. But as Hursh documents, these are exactly the questions that are increasingly ignored in our rush toward neoliberal and "new managerial" policies.

But let us again be honest. The educational crisis is real—especially for the poor and oppressed. Dominant groups have used such "crisis talk" to shift the discussion onto their own terrain.

One of the major reasons for the continuation and growing influence of dominant discourse and policies is that the very nature of our common sense about education is constantly being altered. This is largely the result of the power of particular groups that understand that if they can change the basic ways we think about our society and its institutions—and especially our place in these institutions—they can create a set of policies that will profoundly benefit them more than anyone else. In essence, they have actively engaged in a vast social/pedagogic process, one in which what counts as a good school, good knowledge, good teaching, a good student, and good learning are being radically transformed.

Let me say more about this process. In a large number of countries, a complex alliance and power bloc has been formed that has increasing influence in education and all things social. This power bloc, what I have called *conservative modernization*, is complicated, but its most powerful members are neoliberals, including multiple factions of capital and political leaders and interest groups who are committed to marketized solutions to educational problems, to reductive forms of accountability, and to shifting the blame for very serious inequalities in schooling and the larger society onto teachers and other educators (Apple, 2006).

For many within this alliance, private is necessarily good and public is necessarily bad. Democracy—a key word in how we think about our institutions and our place in them (Foner, 1998)—is reduced to consumption practices. The world becomes a vast supermarket, one in which those with economic and cultural capital are advantaged in nearly every sector of society. Choice in a market replaces more collective and more socially responsive actions. *Thin* democracy replaces *thick* democracy. This demobilizes crucial progressive social movements that have been the driving force behind nearly all of the democratic changes in this society and in our schools. And at the same time neoliberals also increasingly see schools themselves as sites for the generation of profits (see, e.g., Burch, 2009; Ball, 2007; Ball, 2012).

In education, this position is grounded in the belief that the more we marketize, the more we bring corporate models into education, the more we can hold schools, administrators', and teachers' feet to the fire of competition, the better they will be. There actually is very little evidence to support this contention—and a good deal of evidence that it increases inequality (see Apple, 2006; Lipman, 2004; Lipman, 2011). But neoliberalism continues to act as something like a religion in that it seems to be impervious to empirical evidence, even as the crisis that it has created in the economy and in communities constantly documents its failures in every moment of our collective and individual lives.

Certain cities and states sit at the center of these reforms. To name just a few, the list includes Milwaukee, Philadelphia, Chicago, and—the focus of attention of David Hursh's fine book—New York City and New York State. In her well-known and well-received series of volumes on Chicago, Pauline Lipman has powerfully documented the intersections of race and class in producing the destructive effects of neoliberal policies (Lipman, 2004; 2011). Kristen Buras has done a similarly insightful analysis of the distressing situation in New Orleans (Buras, 2015).

Diane Ravitch has also played a key role in these arguments, partly because she is a talented writer with a good deal of visibility but also because, as someone who was a strong and well-placed public proponent of most of these problematic educational policies, her very visible rejection of these same policies gives her voice even more power (see, e.g., Ravitch, 2010; 2014). The fact that she has high-lighted David Hursh's work on her influential blog documents the significance of his arguments.

Hursh thus joins a deservedly well-respected group of critically democratic educational researchers who demonstrate in no uncertain terms what is at stake if we continue down the neoliberal road that has become our new common sense. In the process, he insightfully and honestly examines the complex politics behind these supposed reforms and details the many negative effects they are having. He clearly shows why a focus on New York is important, since what is going on there has serious implications for all of us.

In *Can Education Change Society?* (Apple, 2013), I lay out a range of actions in which the "critical scholar/activist" in education should engage. Among the most important is what I call "bearing witness to negativity"—that is, telling the truth about what is happening in schools and communities given the current empha-sis on neoliberal policies and on measuring anything that moves in classrooms. Another responsibility is documenting the actions of individuals and groups who are acting back, who are defending a more responsive and democratic set of edu-cational policies and practices.

The End of Public Schools engages in both of these things. It does indeed "bear witness" to what is happening. But it doesn't stop there. At the same time, it shows the growth of alternate possibilities for thicker democratic politics around schools and communities. The growing opt-out movement throughout the country, a movement to which David Hursh points, provides a paradigm case. These are groups of parents, community members, teachers, and students who have decided that enough is enough. They are actively refusing to participate in the standardized testing that has now become basically the only measure of school, teacher, and student success (see Hagopian, 2014).

There are many more such possibilities—including the social justice unionism that has been built in places such as Chicago and Vancouver and that challenges neoliberal policies, the creation of democratic schools that work in building com-munities inside and outside of classrooms (see, e.g., Apple and Beane, 2007), and so many more. Journals such as *Rethinking Schools* constantly detail policies and practices that provide reasons for hope rather than the cynicism and blame that now dominate the educational landscape. Yet in order to take advantage of these possibilities, we must continue to shed a bright light on the effects of the neo-liberal and new managerial impulses so prevalent now. What David Hursh documents in *The End of Public Schools* may be discomforting, but it is essential reading for anyone who wants more truly democratic educational reforms.

Michael W. Apple
John Bascom Professor of
Curriculum and Instruction
and Educational Policy Studies
University of Wisconsin–Madison

References

Apple, M. W. (2006). *Educating the "Right" Way: Markets, Standards, God, and Inequality* (2nd ed.). New York: Routledge.

Apple, M. W. (2013). *Can Education Change Society?* New York: Routledge.

Apple, M. W. & Beane, J. A. (Eds.) (2007). *Democratic Schools: Lessons in Powerful Education* (2nd ed.). Portsmouth, NH: Heinemann.

Ball, S. (2007). *Education plc: Understanding Private Sector Participation in Public Sector Education.* New York: Routledge.

Ball, S. (2012). *Global Education Inc.: New Policy Networks and the Neo-liberal Imaginary.* New York: Routledge.

Buras, K. (2015). *Charter Schools, Race, and Urban Space: Where the Market Meets Grassroots Resistance.* New York: Routledge.

Burch, P. (2009). *Hidden Markets: The New Education Privatization.* New York: Routledge.

Foner, E. (1998). *The Story of American Freedom.* New York: Norton.

Hagopian, J. (Ed.) (2014). *More Than a Score: The New Uprising Against High-Stakes Testing.* Chicago: Haymarket Books.

Lipman, P. (2004). *High Stakes Education: Inequality, Globalization, and Urban School Reform.* New York: Routledge.

Lipman, P. (2011). *The New Political Economy of Education: Neoliberalism, Race, and the Right to the City.* New York: Routledge.

Ravitch, D. (2010). *The Death and Life of the Great American School System.* New York: Basic Books.

Ravitch, D. (2014). *Reign of Error: The Hoax of the Privatization Movement and the Danger to America's Public Schools.* New York: Vintage Books.

ACKNOWLEDGMENTS

The person with the greatest influence on my political education has been Michael Apple. Reading Michael's *Ideology and Curriculum* (1979) in the early 1980s changed my life. In response, I sent Michael a letter introducing myself and began soon thereafter as his doctoral advisee at the University of Wisconsin-Madison. Over the last 35 years, he has been a model of how to use critical analysis to change the world.

While at the University of Wisconsin I was lucky to get to know and learn from many doctoral students who either preceded me, were contemporaries, or followed me. These included: Marie Brennan (thank you for your inexhaustible enthusiasm) and Pauline Lipman and Tom Pedroni, who know more about the politics of education in Chicago and Detroit (respectively) than anyone else I know. Among those from whom I continue to learn but who are no longer with us: Susan Noffke and Landon Beyer.

Former University of Rochester Provost Ralph Kuncl granted me a sabbatical in the spring of 2014 that allowed me to travel for nine weeks to New Zealand and Australia where I gave speeches to teachers' unions and university students and faculty and tried out many of the ideas in this book. The sabbatical also provided me with time to read and write. On that trip, I renewed valuable friendships with Bob Lingard, Fazal Rizvi, Marc Pryn, John Smyth, Martin Thrupp, Deborah Fraser, Tina Beasley, Michael Peters, David Berliner, and Lew Zipin. Other international colleagues whose work has significantly influenced me include Susan Robertson, Roger Dale, Stephen Ball, Sally Tomlinson, and Meg Maquire.

In addition to U.S. colleagues mentioned above, I am thankful for the inspiration and guidance provided by Sheila Macrine, Joao Paraskeva, Ken Saltman, Marilyn Cochran-Smith, Christine Sleeter, Linda McNeil, Angelia Valenzeula, and Stephen Fleury.

I am most grateful to the students in my classes at the Warner School at the University of Rochester, in particular the masters and undergraduate students who enroll in my course that focuses on the history and politics of education in the United States and where I often first try out my analyses. I also thank the doctoral students who participated in my fall 2014 class on "globalization in education," where we applied many of the concepts described in this book, such as social imaginary, corporate managerialism, and heterarchy.

I have also learned and continue to learn from my many doctoral advisees. Among them is Joseph Henderson, who recently coedited with me a special issue of *Environmental Education Research* on "environmental education within a neoliberal climate." In addition, Catherine Compton-Lilly and Rebecca Goldstein are past advisees who became longtime colleagues.

However, this book is not merely an analysis of education policy but part of a larger effort to change it. Over the last 20 years, I have worked with teachers, parents, and administrators who work hard every day to improve schools through political activism. These include members of the Coalition for Justice in Education and the leaders of several local unions, including the Rochester Teachers Association and Spencerport Teachers Association. I have also benefitted by working alongside educational activists Bill Cala (former superintendent of the Fairport School District), Dan Drmacich (former principal of School Without Walls in the Rochester City School District), and Mary Adams (Rochester City School District Board Member).

Lastly, during the last fifteen years, Camille Martina has been coconspirator, coresearcher, coauthor, confidant, and spouse. We began researching and writing about high-stakes testing and the corporate reform agenda based on her experience as a secondary English teacher in the Rochester City School District. Later, we added research and teaching on environmental health based on her second career researching toxins in the environment, which resulted in a coauthored book on teaching environmental health to children. She has encouraged me to reach further and to accomplish more than I imagined I could. This book would not have been possible without her support.

1

THE DEMISE OF THE PUBLIC IN PUBLIC SCHOOLS

We may be witnessing the end of public education in the United States. Not in the sense that public funding of schools will cease, although funding is likely to decrease. Rather, we will see the end of public education in two ways: first, more public funding will go toward privately managed charter schools and less toward publicly governed schools. Second, education will be less public in that students, teachers, school and district committees, and elected school boards will have less say over education policy. Instead, policy will be made by unelected and unaccountable individuals, corporations, and organizations, such as the Bill and Melinda Gates Foundation; Pearson Education; state commissioners of education; the federal secretary of education; and Teach for America.

In New York, as I will detail, teachers and parents are increasingly at odds with the policies of the State Department of Education and the federal government. Recent federal policies, such as No Child Left Behind (NCLB) and Race to the Top (RTTT), impose standardized testing on students and limit teachers' choices regarding curriculum content and pedagogy. Moreover, for almost the last two decades the New York State Department of Education, under the leadership of a commissioner and the directives from the Board of Regents, have manipulated tests scores to portray students as succeeding or failing depending on what best serves their own political ends (Winerip, 2011).

Most recently, as I will show, Governor Cuomo has hijacked education policy for his own political purposes. In response to the millions of dollars he has received from financiers and other supporters of charter schools, he introduced and signed into law regulations benefiting charter school investors. He also introduced and signed legislation intended to portray public schools and public school teachers as failing with the goal of ending what he calls "the public school monopoly" (Taylor, 2015).

My opening sentence is not meant to be hyperbolic. Rather, it is intended to alert the reader that public education has been radically transformed over the last few decades based on a corporate model of market competition, with quantitative evaluations of students, teachers, schools, and school districts based on students' scores on standardized tests. Teachers have decreasing input on assessment and curriculum as those tasks are handed over to corporations. Moreover, both state and federal governments are pushing for converting public schools into publicly funded but privately managed schools. New Orleans has closed all its public schools and replaced them with charter schools (Buras, 2014, 2015). Atlanta, Georgia, plans to replace all of its public schools with charter schools (Atlanta Public Schools, 2015).

We need to understand that the education reforms are not minor changes in how schools are administered, or how tests and curriculum are created, or how teachers are evaluated. Instead, the current reforms have transformed the purpose of schooling, teaching, and learning. The curriculum is being reduced to what will be tested, teaching reduced to implementing lessons designed to resemble the test questions and often scripted by someone else, and learning reduced to test-taking strategies and memorizing for the test. Good teachers are retiring early or finding other jobs, and enrollments in teacher education programs are declining. In the Rochester-area teacher education institutions, enrollments in teacher certification programs declined on average by about 70% from 2008 to 2012, the most recent years for which data are available (Integrated Postsecondary Education Data System, 2014).

Moreover, the original rationale for charter schools has been transformed. Charter schools, as Kahlenberg and Potter (2014–2015) remind us, were originally proposed by the American Federation of Teachers, the union representing most urban teachers, as a way for teachers and community members to collaborate in creating innovative publicly funded and governed schools that would inspire reform. Instead, charter schools have evolved into privately managed schools that generally promote authoritarian models of teaching and treat teachers as commodities to be used for a few years and then replaced with younger and less expensive teachers (Taylor, 2015). In addition, in most states (laws governing charter schools vary by state, and charter schools differ from one another) charter schools, on average, have increased racial and economic segregation, enroll smaller percentages of students with disabilities or who are English Language Learners, and have failed to keep pace with traditional public schools in educating students (see Ravitch, 2013, chapter 16, "The Contradictions of Charters").

Even worse, the increasing use of standardized tests to hold students, teachers, and schools accountable, along with the privatization of schools through charters and the takeover of education governance by unelected and unaccountable individuals, nongovernmental organizations, and corporations, has failed to improve educational outcomes or decrease economic and racial inequalities. There is little evidence that scores are improving at the rate they did prior to the reforms

(Ravitch, 2013; Winerip, 2011). Moreover, if we look at schooling beyond test scores, the narrowing and simplifying of curriculum has undermined learning. At its best, states Giroux (2012), education should promote students' "analytical abilities, thoughtful exchange and a willingness to view knowledge as a resource for informed modes of individual and social agency" (p. 1). Instead, education based on corporate-created assessments and curriculum results in an "education deficit" where the public suffers "from a growing inability to think critically question authority, be reflective, weigh evidence, discriminate between reasoned arguments and opinions, listen across differences and engage in mutually informing relationship between private problems and broader public issues" (Giroux, 2012, p. 1).

No Child Left Behind, Race to the Top, the rise of charter schools, and the increasing privatization and corporatization of public education are not accidental developments. Rather, I argue that the current debate over the direction of public education exemplifies a larger debate occurring in the United States and globally: on the one hand, we can continue pursuing the neoliberal agenda that aims to create a society in which decisions about how we are to live are made through unregulated markets, with a diminished governmental role as what was once public is privatized. In such a system, students and teachers are infinitely examined (Foucault, 1979; Hanson, 1993) and are held accountable through an "accountability synopticism" (Simmonds and Webb, 2013, p. 21). On the other hand, we can pursue what I will call a social liberal democratic agenda in which the government plays its required role in the creation and development of markets, provides services that are best provided through the government, creates schools as learning communities that support the development of trusting and caring relationships, and aims to create democratic institutions and structures so that everyone has opportunities to participate in democratic processes.

In suggesting that we face a choice between two visions of society, both shaped by different views of the appropriate economic and government structures and practices, I am asserting that educators need to become familiar with economic theory and history. In fact, we cannot leave economics to the economists, who, for the most part, assume that free market capitalism is the best of all possible worlds and the role of the economist is to develop models to increase the market's efficiency and produce evermore goods and services (Block & Somers, 2014; Hursh, 2014). Instead, I argue, educators cannot leave economic theory, policies, and practices to economists but must understand economic theory and policies so as to demystify them and the role they play in creating the world in which we live.

Therefore, to introduce the debate, I begin this chapter with a brief historical overview of social democratic liberalism as initially promoted under the administration of Franklin Delano Roosevelt and neoliberal economic and political theory that arose in response. Then I will turn to providing examples of neoliberal education reform that has occurred at the state level, with New York as the primary example, and at the federal level. However, I will show that it is no longer sufficient to describe education and other policies as created at the local, state, and federal levels. Instead, policy is more often made outside of the governmental sphere as powerful groups, corporations, and individuals have gained inordinate access to both public officials and the media in ways that the public has not. Therefore, in the last part of the chapter, I will propose that democracy and social justice requires that we respond to the neoliberal agenda by (1) promoting a vision for society that opposes neoliberalism; (2) researching, publicizing, and working against the increasing social and economic inequality in our society and schools; and (3) creating political practices and institutional structures that promote democratic participation at the local, state, federal, and national levels.

Situating the Current Neoliberal Reforms within Three Conflicting Conceptions of Society

Classical liberalism emerged in the 1600–1700s in England with the Petition of Rights of 1628 and later in the United States with the Declaration of Independence. It remained the dominant economic and political structure in the United States and Western Europe through World War I and into the economic boom of the 1920s that was soon to go bust. Classical liberalism aimed to

> [S]afeguard the freedoms of the individual against the arbitrary power of the sovereign's rule. Their freedoms included: government by the consent of the governed, the natural rights of citizens to private property which must be protected against infraction by any arbitrary acts of government, periodic popular elections to regulate the power of the ruling body through regular appraisal of the requirement to rule responsibly, and citizens right to revolt against the despotic rule who violate their natural rights.
>
> (Olssen, Codd, & O'Neill, 2004, p. 80)

Because classical liberalism valued individual freedom over government intervention, ideally, government should have as small a role as possible in directing the economy and society. Consequently, public services, such as public schools (until the rise of the common school), public universities, pensions, and health care were nonexistent. In addition, as the economy experienced booms and busts, governments theoretically could not respond and, at least in the case of recessions, did not practically have sufficient revenue to do so.

However, with the onset of the Great Depression in 1929 in the United States, President Hoover's cuts in the federal budget both prolonged the economic slump and failed to provide basic services to the unemployed and poor. Franklin Roosevelt, soon after becoming president, created policies based on the economic theories of John Maynard Keynes, theories sometimes referred to as social democratic liberalism. Under Keynesian theory, the government has an obligation to intervene in the economy to create jobs and reduce the negative impact of economic recessions and depressions—and to do so even if it creates a budget deficit, on the reasoning that once the economy recovers, the budget deficit can be reduced or eliminated. Roosevelt transformed the relationship between the federal government, the economy, and citizens as he pushed through Congress programs that would give people jobs (Works Progress Administration and the Civilian Conservation Corps) and provide financial security for the elderly and widowed (Social Security). Just as importantly, Roosevelt signed into law regulations such as the Glass-Steagal Act (1933), which limited banks' ability to make risky loans, and programs such as the Federal Deposit Insurance Company (FDIC), which insures deposits, therefore reducing people's fear that they would lose their savings if their bank went bankrupt.

As beneficial as these policies were, as Block and Somers (2014) point out, "market fundamentalists" (p. 3) remained convinced that markets and not the government should determine social and economic policies. Economists and politicians began to develop alternatives to Roosevelt's social democratic liberalism with, as I will describe later, alternative conceptions coming from two centers of neoliberal thought: the Mont Pelerin Society founded in 1947 under the leadership of Frederick von Hayek in Austria, and economists at the University of Chicago headed, after 1946, by Milton Friedman (Peck, 2010, p. 17). Some, like Hayek, feared that the social democratic policies becoming dominant in the United States and the United Kingdom after World War II would result in a planned society modeled after the communist Soviet Union. This fear is reflected in the title of his most renowned book, *The Road to Serfdom* (1944).

Even with the rise of the two centers of neoliberal theorizing, neoliberalism remained a subordinate ideology as Keynesian economic policies produced a growing economy. The policies of the 1950s and '60s raised the income and living standards of the middle class, which increased consumer confidence and consumption and led to increased corporate profits. As Block and Somers (2014) write,

> [M]ost of the business community in the United States had made its peace with Keynesianism by recognizing the benefits of a substantial role for government in the economy. In the Johnson and Nixon Administrations, business leaders supported initiatives to expand public provisions of health care and social provisioning, as well as acquiesced to new environmental and consumer protections.
>
> (p. 204)

Unfortunately, as Block and Somers (2014), Harvey (2005), and Johnson and Salle (2004) point out, and I later expand on, in the 1970s, corporate profits began to decline for a variety of reasons, including the increasing globalized market; the formation of the Organization of the Petroleum Producing Countries (OPEC), which subsequently raised oil prices; and a federal budget deficit resulting from funding the Vietnam War.

Corporations began to forge an assault on social democratic policies by bringing neoliberal policies into the mainstream and organizing institutions that would provide the ideological basis beyond University of Chicago economists. A central figure in promoting a neoliberal political response was Lewis Powell, a corporate lawyer for Philip Morris, the cigarette manufacturer, who was to be soon a Nixon appointee to the Supreme Court. Powell (1971), in a famous memo to the Chamber of Commerce, urged the business community to push back against their "anti-capitalist" critics and to move forward in creating organizations that would promote "free enterprise" (Block & Somers, 2014, p. 200).

The Powell memo transformed politics in the United States as wealthy businessmen (the lists I have seen include no women) used their wealth to create numerous neoliberal and neoconservative think tanks. Johnson and Salle, in *Responding to the Attack on Public Education and Teacher Unions* (2004), detail who funded which organization or foundation, too many to list here, but People for the American Way, in *Buying a Movement* (Egan, 1996) reveals that:

> Five foundations stand out from the rest: the Lynde and Harry Bradley Foundation, the Koch Family foundations [whose money founded the Cato Institute but who are now pumping $889 million into the 2016 campaign to support "deregulation, tax cuts and smaller government" (Confessore, 2015)], the John M. Olin Foundation, the Scaife Family foundations and the Adolf Coors Foundation [the American Heritage Foundation]. Each has helped fund a range of far-right programs, including some of the most politically charged work of the last several years.
>
> (p. 3)

Business leaders formed an alliance with cultural and religious conservatives (Kruse, 2015) to roll back the social democratic agenda and return to the classical liberal economic structure and policies that existed pre-Roosevelt. This turn in American politics reflects the dominant role that foundations have come to play in promoting particular policies. As I will later argue, numerous foundations play the key role in supporting the current neoliberal educational reforms, including the Common Core State Standards, charter schools, and vouchers, such as the Gates Foundation, the Walton Foundation, and others. In fact, the major players in determining education policy are wealthy foundations that have no obligation to be transparent or democratic.

The increasing influence of wealthy individuals and foundations highlights some ways in which neoliberalism is and is not like social democratic liberalism nor classical liberalism, with which it might be compared and confused. First, because they share the word liberal, neoliberalism is sometimes confused with social democratic liberalism, which is often associated with the notion of cultural liberalism, and the political and economic policies of Democratic politicians such as President Lyndon Johnson's "great society." Neoliberalism is the opposite of social democratic liberalism.

Nor is, if we take the idea of free markets seriously, neoliberalism a return to classical liberalism. As described previously, the ability of wealthy individuals, foundations, and corporations to intervene throughout society shifts control away from individuals' operation in the marketplace to the wealthy. What has developed in the United States is not free markets but a plutocracy, or rule by the rich (Sachs, 2014).

Since the notion of liberal has taken on many contradictory meanings, it might be prudent to drop the term all together. Block and Somers (2014) do not use the term neoliberal but offer what is perhaps a more accurate description of those who support such policies, describing them as *market fundamentalists* for their almost religious faith in markets. But, because neoliberal is the more common term, I will use the term neoliberal more often than market fundamentalist. However, I will sometimes use the latter term to emphasize that the notion reflects an almost unshakeable faith that free markets are always preferable to government intervention (Crouch, 2011). In addition, like Block and Somers (2014), I will argue that markets free of regulation as described by neoliberals cannot exist, nor can they be free of governmental and corporate intervention, and that markets cannot respond to most of our economic and social needs (Sachs, 2015).

Neoliberals aim to limit government's role in society by believing that it is always more efficient for individuals and corporations to make decisions within competitive markets free of governmental regulation. This faith that markets are always more efficient and responsive provides one rationale for recent education reforms such as charter schools, vouchers, and privatization, in which, as ideally proposed, schools compete with one another for students. The notion that students and their families should choose between competing schools also provides a rationale for standardized testing: to give students and their families "objective" data regarding the quality of the schools.

Neoliberals also conceptualize the relationship between the individual and society differently than under Keynesian conceptions. For Roosevelt and other social democrats, cooperation and equality will result in a society in which individuals benefit the most. In fact, recent research by Pickett and Wilkinson (2011) demonstrates that the more economically equal a society, the healthier individuals are across all social classes.

As implied previously, neoliberalism undermines democracy both in theoretically reducing decision making to the market place and in practice to those who have the economic and political power to intervene in the political process. Furthermore, as I will describe, where education policy is made has shifted up the geopolitical scale from the local and state to the federal, national, and international (corporations, foundations, and nongovernmental organizations), disempowering those who lack the financial and political clout to affect policy decisions at the upper levels.

By situating the current corporate education reform movement within the context of two visions of society—Keynesian social democracy or neoliberalism—I will show how the recent corporate reforms reflect the neoliberal social vision. I will use the current conflicts in education occurring at the local, state, national, federal, and international levels as case studies of the larger societal conflict over what kind of society we want: a society where government is marginalized and democracy is limited to choosing between the options that corporations provide *or* a society that builds on Dewey's vision of democratic communities in which schools prepare students to be critical, democratic decision makers.

How Neoliberal Education Policy Undermines Democracy and Equality

Teacher evaluations have historically been conducted at the school and district levels. However, currently in New York, as part of the agreement to receive funding under Race to the Top (RTTT), 40% of a teacher's evaluation is based on their students' scores on standardized tests created and graded by Pearson Education. More recently, Governor Andrew Cuomo proposed that 85% of a teacher's evaluation be based on the standardized tests and teacher observations conducted by examiners chosen by the state, therefore almost entirely eliminating the role of the school district in which the teacher is employed (Lovett, 2014). The legislature amended the proposal to permit observers from the same district if they taught or were administrators in a different school, a requirement that many small school districts will not be able to meet (Strauss, 2015).

Moreover, because decisions are increasingly influenced if not made outside the traditional political process by persons who are unelected and unaccountable, the public is sidelined from the decision-making process. Instead, those with power and money gain access to and have leverage over commissioners of education, legislators, governors, and like-minded nongovernmental organizations and foundations. Some of the most powerful and wealthy individuals and organizations include:

- Bill Gates, the world's richest person at $79.2 billion (Dolan & Kroll, 2015).
- The Gates Foundation, which in 2013 had $41 billion in assets and awarded 13.2 billion in grants. The foundation distributed more almost six times move in grants assets than the next largest foundation. Whose purpose is other than providing financial assistance to purchase pharmaceuticals, such as the Bristol-Myers Squibb Patient Assistance Program (Foundation Center, 2014).
- The Walton Family Foundation, which supports creating charter schools and just funded busing some 10,000 charter school teachers and students to Albany, New York, to urge passage of legislation that would increase the number of and funding for charter schools (Campbell, 2015).
- Pearson, the world's largest education company.

- Neoliberal foundations such as Teach for America that prepare teachers in six weeks over the summer to teach for a few years and then to engage in efforts to privatize education. Teach for America is a global organization with programs in 36 countries.

Others have conducted in-depth studies on the changing nature of philanthropy in general (Saltman, 2010) and The Gates Foundation in particular (Kovacs, 2011). Still others have looked at the increasing role of corporations in steering policy and developing assessments and curriculum (Ball, 2012). In this book, I do not attempt to articulate the complicated, varied, and dense connections between foundations such as Gates or corporations such as Pearson. Rather, my aim is to describe the ways in which neoliberal and market fundamentalist ideologies have transformed education by turning over policy making to the rich and powerful who are generally unelected and unaccountable. While most schools districts are still governed by locally elected school boards, the boards make fewer decisions than before as assessment and curriculum decisions are made by corporations and individuals who are not members of the community and have political and economic rather than educational interests.

The Gates Foundation uses its wealth, power, and political connections to promote its preferred causes. For example, the Common Core State Standards would not exist if Gates had not provided "millions to the National Governors Association, to the Council on Chief School Officers, to Achieve and to Student Achievement Partners" (Strauss, 2014a). As of March 2014, the Gates Foundation has provided $2.3 billion to support creating and implementing the Common Core State Standards (Hassard, 2014), with more than 1,800 grants to organizations ranging from teachers' unions to state departments of education to political groups that have pushed the Common Core into 45 states, with little transparency and next to no public review. Education blogger Mercedes Schneider has posted a four-part series detailing which organizations received how much to support the CCSS (Schneider, 2013).

Not only has the Gates Foundation almost single-handedly funded the creation, endorsement, and implementation of the CCSS, they directly influence policy by placing personnel in positions of power. In addition, and most disturbingly, the Gates Foundation and other foundations promoting school privatization are the primary source for personnel in the United States Department of Education, including former officers (Gates, 2009; Hursh, 2015). Schneider recently revealed in an analysis of eight key Department of Education appointees that they all came from organizations promoting privatizing schools. One came directly from the Gates Foundation, and several came from the Gates-funded New Schools Venture Fund, including the undersecretary of education, Ted Mitchell (Schneider, 2014b).

Besides spending billions on promoting the CCSS, and essentially sharing administrative staff with the U.S. Department of Education, Bill Gates benefits from politicians seeking out his views even though he has no formal background in education, nor does he have expertise in his other initiatives of global health and agriculture. In March 2014, Bill Gates and David Brooks (Schneider, 2014a) a journalist who erroneously believes that the Common Core State Standards are a state and not federal initiative (Brooks, 2014), gave an invited dinner address to 80 U.S. senators where they extolled the virtues of the CCSS.

Yet, while Gates and the other corporate reformers have spent literally billions on improving education in the United States and touted that it is education and not income redistribution that will reduce inequality, education, while continuing to improve (as least according to scores on the National Assessment of Educational Progress), is not improving at the rate it was pre-No Child Left Behind (Ravitch, 2013).

In addition, economic inequality and poverty have increased. Childhood poverty in the United States has increased to an extent that it has the second highest level of child poverty among 35 industrialized nations, second only to Romania (Children's Defense Fund, 2014, p. 16). Similarly, the Southern Education Foundation (2014) reports that over half (51%) of all students attending public schools are eligible for free or reduced lunch, indicating that their families are low income. Therefore, more than half of our public school students live in poverty (Rich, 2015).

In New York, where as I will show the State Department of Education and, now, the governor have made high-stakes standardized testing central to the education "reform" movement, the plight of the children has only worsened. The Civil Rights Project of UCLA reports that, based on the most recent data, New York has the highest rate of segregated schools in the United States. The report states, "Black and Latino students in the state had the highest concentration in intensely-segregated public schools (less than 10% White enrollment), the lowest exposure to White students, and the most uneven distribution with White students across schools" (Kucsera, 2014), with schools in metropolitan Rochester and Buffalo classified as highly segregated (Civil Rights Project, 2014).

Not only are the Rochester and Buffalo schools highly segregated, but also both cities have extremely high rates of poverty and childhood poverty. Rochester's poverty rate is the second highest in the United States among cities with a population of 200,000 or more, with 55.2% of children living in poverty and 35.4% of residents overall. Buffalo fares only slightly better as the city with the fourth highest childhood poverty rate (50.6%) and fifth highest rate overall (31.4%) (Sharp, 2014).

Given all of the above—that our schools are not improving at the same rate as previous to the corporate reforms, that our scores on the Programme for International Student Assessment (PISA) exams have been trending downward (Darling-Hammond, 2014), that our society and schools are becoming more segregated and unequal—how have the so-called education reformers succeeded in achieving their agenda and marginalizing all others? What might be done in response? How do we need to think about the relationship between education, the economy, and democracy?

To answer these questions, I focus on the last two decades of education reforms in New York, situated within Bush's No Child Left Behind and Obama's Race to the Top programs. New York is worth examining because it epitomizes some of the shifts in governance and education policy over the last several decades.

First, the governor, Andrew Cuomo, has intervened in education policy to an unprecedented degree in which the governor and the state legislature, not the regents, who are the legitimate governing body regarding education policy, are determining how and on what basis teachers are to be evaluated. This same politicization of teachers and schools is occurring in most other states, as described by Buras (2014, 2015) regarding the destruction of the teachers' union and public schools in New Orleans, by Pedroni (2011) regarding the state of Michigan's takeover and privatization of the Detroit Public Schools, and by Ladd (2015) regarding the proposal to essentially end public schools in Texas by setting up a parallel system to fund private schools.

Second, I also describe the shift from government to governance and the all-important influence that unelected and unaccountable organizations and individuals, such as the Bill and Melinda Gates Foundation, the Tisch Foundation, and Pearson Education, have on education policy. Furthermore, education policies and administration are increasingly guided by data, including standardized test scores. Ball (2015) refers to this shift as "the tyranny of numbers" that reduces the human component of teaching and learning.

Third, teachers' unions came to power as part of the civil rights movement in the 1960s. The American Federation of Teachers was founded in Chicago 1916 and won few major victories until after World War II. Then, under the leadership of Albert Shanker, head of the New York City local United Federation of Teachers (UFT), the teachers engaged in a one-day strike to secure the right to collectively bargain. The UFT continued to dominate the AFT as Shanker was elected president of the AFT in 1974, and his successors in the UFT also followed him to become president of the AFT (AFT n.d.).

For the last 30 years of the twentieth century, the two teachers' unions in New York—the National Education Association (NEA) and the AFT—gained significant power to influence education policy. However, in New York, as elsewhere around the United States, teachers' unions have been under attack as "special interests" that need to be eliminated or marginalized for the corporate reforms to succeed.

Fourth, both Republicans and Democrats have taken up the corporate reform agenda. While neoliberal ideals promoting free markets and decreasing government's responsibility for social welfare appeal to most Republicans and members of groups such as the Tea Party, the corporate reform agenda is being promoted in historically Democratic states (Michigan, Illinois, and New York) and cities (Chicago). Examining how education policy evolved in New York, especially given that Andrew Cuomo has embraced an education agenda that opposed that of his father, Mario Cuomo, former three-term social democratic governor of

New York, provides insight into how it is that neoliberalism and market fundamentalism has been taken up by Democrats (Cassidy, 2015).

A Brief History of How High-Stakes Testing and Privatization Came to Dominate New York's Schools

Since 1866, New York has been giving and requiring students to pass several standardized high school Regents exams to earn a Regents diploma, which was more difficult than the alternative local diploma (Beadie, 1999). My own experience as a high school student in the 1960s was that the score on each subject area exam was added to a student's grades for the four quarters to determine their overall average for the year. Furthermore, as long as a student passed the required minimum number of Regents courses with their respective exams, they received the Regents diploma. So, while important, the Regents exams were not high stakes. One could fail the Regents exam and still pass the course or fail a few Regents exams and still earn a Regents diploma.

But, in 1995, the New York Commissioner of Education Richard Mills and the Board of Regents adopted policies requiring students to pass five Regents exams, one each in English, science, and math and two in social studies, beginning with English in 1996 and adding on an additional subject each year (Natriello & Pallas, 1999, p. 9). Because failure to pass any *one* of the exams prohibited earning a Regents degree and the alternative non-Regents track was being eliminated, students who passed all their classes but could not pass *one* exam, the exams became high stakes.

As I will describe in chapter 3, this requirement was highly contested, particularly by the 20 high schools that were part of the Performance Standards Consortium, schools that had been granted a waiver permitting them to grant Regents diplomas without students taking the tests by the previous commissioner, Tom Sobol (Hursh, 2008). The federal government did not interfere in testing policies until 2002, when the federal government passed the No Child Left Behind (NCLB) as part of the Elementary and Secondary Education Act and significantly expanded their reach into public schools beyond anything previously known. Indeed, many argue that NCLB and later RTTT are unconstitutional because the United States Constitution does not explicitly include education as a responsibility of the federal government and explicitly states that anything not listed in the Constitution is reserved for the states. The most well-known aspect of NCLB is the requirement that schools evaluate students, schools, and districts based on students' scores on the reading and mathematics tests in grades three through eight. The test scores are to be disaggregated along several dimensions, including race and ethnicity, to assess whether the school is making Adequate Yearly Progress (AYP).

AYP is not based on whether and to what degree the school's test scores have improved but, instead, the percentage of students who achieve the passing score. The minimum percentage of students required to achieve the passing score increases each year, starting low in 2002, NCLB's first year, and gradually increasing until 2014 when 100% of students are required to pass the exam.

Since achieving AYP is based on what percentage of students pass the test each year and not whether their scores improve, NCLB has the perverse effect of harming schools with large percentages of students living in poverty. Since students' test scores are closely related to family income, schools with large percentages of students living in poverty, which is any city in New York, are unlikely to have a sufficient percentage of students pass the test. Moreover, since the percentage of students required to pass the test increases each year, schools with large percentages of children living in poverty do *not* achieve AYP if their passing rate fails to increase sufficiently to rise above the ascending line. On the other hand, financially wealthy suburban districts that begin with a passing rate above the minimum threshold will continue to make AYP, even if their passing rate declines, as long as they remains above the minimum threshold. Therefore, while progress is commonly equated with the notion of improving, under NCLB, can have declining passing rates and be determined to be making progress while poor schools can have increasing passing rates and be classified as not making progress. Of course, it is almost impossible for any school to achieve the 100% passing rate as required by 2014, which would have led to almost all of the schools failing, if it were not, as I shall show, for Obama's waivers.

However irrational it seems to develop criteria that will result in almost all schools failing, it has two political advantages. First, George W. Bush signed into law a bill that resulted in all schools failing not during his administration but during the 2014 presidency, making that president and political party look like failures. As we shall see, Obama's RTTT is an effort to avoid that outcome. Second, promoters of school privatization could use data on the increasing number of failing schools as part of the rationale for why schools need to be privatized.

While standardized tests and accountability have been the most discussed aspects of NCLB, some of the other provisions in the thousand-page act are worth mentioning. NCLB imposed additional requirements in various subject areas, most significantly in literacy, where districts were required to choose curriculum from a limited set of literacy approaches (Chistianarkis, 2015). Another contested requirement of NCLB is the requirement that school districts hand over their graduating seniors' contact information to military recruiters unless parents explicitly prohibit it in writing (Bracey, 2002).

Another aspect of the corporate reform movement has been the effort by city mayors to either disband or disempower locally elected school boards of trustees so as to implement more testing and privatization. For example, in 2002, New York City Mayor Michael Bloomberg, a wealthy business entrepreneur who is founder and owner of Bloomberg LP, the "world's leading financial news and information company" (Bloomberg, 2015), sought and was granted by the New York State Assembly mayoral control over the city's schools. While he did not disband the school board, he threatened and on occasion removed board members who voted against his wishes. He appointed Joel Klein, CEO of the global media giant Bertelsman, as schools chancellor. As described by Wohlstetter and Houston (2015), Klein and Bloomberg "began to restructure the entire school district, based on principles of efficiency, entrepreneurship, and innovation" (p. 1). Bloomberg and Klein both supported increasing the number of charter schools in the city and using the standardized tests required under NCLB to evaluate students, teachers, and schools, including determining whether students should be promoted to the next grade.

In New York, therefore, the number and consequences of standardized testing increased in several stages: first the regents required that high school students pass five exams in order to graduate, then NCLB spread standardized testing in reading and math from grades three through eight. Next, Mayor Bloomberg raised the stakes on testing in New York City. Finally, the federal secretary of education, Arne Duncan, and President Obama imposed more constraints and privatization on schools. They accomplished this by the Race to the Top (RTTT) program or, for states that did not "win" the RTTT competition, by granting states waivers from achieving the 100% passing rate on NCLB's tests if they agreed to RTTT's testing and curriculum requirements.

RTTT, as will be obvious, was (it has now ended for lack of funding) a great disappointment to critics of more standardized testing, was connected to higher stakes, and had more privatization via charter schools. Many, including myself, had hoped that if elected Obama would reverse Bush's federal policies and interpreted his hiring of Linda Darling-Hammond, Stanford University professor of education, as his education advisor during his campaign as a sign that he might do so. However, when Darling-Hammond resigned from the administration and Obama appointed Arne Duncan, who was previously the CEO of the Chicago Public Schools and led their corporate reform makeover, hope died (Hursh 2015).

NCLB, or more formally the Elementary and Secondary Education Act, ESEA, remained in force as law until April 2015, about which I will say more in the last chapter. To avoid the embarrassing consequences of not achieving the NCLB's 2014 deadline of a 100% passing rate, Obama used funds from the American Recovery and Reinvestment Act (ARRA) of 2009, therefore circumventing approaching a divided Congress for funding. There were at least two incentives behind the RTTT initiative. First, states that successfully competed for and were awarded RTTT funding no longer had to comply with NCLB, therefore reducing the number of schools that would fail during the Obama administration, in fact shifting attention away from NCLB to RTTT. RTTT also abandoned the long-term existing federal policy that favored funding districts "based on the proportion of students who were poor" (Ravitch, 2013, p. 15).

Second, given that states were suffering significant revenue reductions as they emerged out of the worst recession since the Great Depression of the 1930s, Obama could encourage states to accept the Common Core curriculum and assessments, put into law new regulations to increase the number of charter schools permitted in the state, and increase the use of standardized test scores in evaluating teachers.

If states were hoping that RTTT funding would benefit their schools, they were likely to be disappointed. For most school districts in New York, the cost of putting RTTT requirements into practice exceeded the amounts received. For example, districts had to develop and implement assessments in every subject and grade and evaluate teachers and principals through, at minimum, two observations a year. In Monroe County (not counting the city of Rochester), school districts received $127,000 over four years or just under $32,000 a year. Or, dividing the amount given to districts by the number of children in the state, each district received $33.50 per student per year (J. Siegle, Executive Director of the Monroe County School Boards Association, personal communication with the author, March 12, 2012).

One rural Rochester district itemized the expense of implementing RTTT. The total RTTT funding the district will received over four years was $20,000. However, a district administrator calculated that in the *first year* they spent $157,346 on RTTT-mandated activities and technology updates that they would not have spent otherwise. She also calculated that they spent $310,045 on activities for which they might have spent the funds otherwise (Williams, 2013). Rather than aiding already underfunded schools, RTTT reduces the funding available for teachers, professional development, and educational resources. Consequently, states ceded control over their curriculum and assessments with the hope of receiving additional funding, only to find that Duncan and his privateers were now in control of their school districts.

Diane Ravitch (2013) summarizes the consequences of RTTT, stating that most states are now required:

> [T]o adopt "college and career-readiness standards," which most states understood as the Common Core State Standards (CCSS) that were funded mainly by the Gates Foundation and promoted by the Obama administration. They had to agree to test students to measure progress toward meeting the goals of college and career readiness; these were the tests funded by the Obama administration to assess the Common Core standards. They had to agree to submit their standards and assessments to the U.S. Department of Education for review. They had to agree to evaluate teachers and principals using student test scores as a significant part of their evaluation. They had to agree to establish a system of recognizing schools as "reward," "focus," and "priority" schools, which were the lowest performing. They had to develop a plan to establish measurable objectives for all their schools.
>
> (p. 282)

A further requirement not mentioned by Ravitch but with significant fiscal implications for financially strapped schools is that students are required to complete exams not on pencil and paper tests but on computers, adding costs for school districts that need to purchase additional technology.

Even with all these requirements and knowing that the number of awards were limited, states, with already tight education budgets now stretched to the limit by the ongoing recession, fell over one another passing legislation linking teacher pay to test scores and authorizing charter schools. As a result, some states passed sweeping legislation that created radical changes in their education systems but, because they were not awarded RTTT funding, did so without receiving any of the funding promised. In a climate of financial desperation, bribery works. Moreover, since RTTT was funded using stimulus money (ARRA) to alleviate the financial recession, after four years, when ARRA funded ended, so did funding for RTTT (Strauss, 2014b).

RTTT then expanded the testing required by NCLB to include not only reading and math in grades three through eight but to evaluate every teacher via a test score on either a standardized test or a test assessing the subject Standards of Learning (SOL). This resulted in some odd arrangements, such as having first grade teachers' evaluations based on student scores on reading tests taken in third grade. RTTT expanded evaluation through high-stakes testing to every student in every class and for every teacher (Leonardatos & Zahedi, 2014).

In New York, tests scores, as I will show in chapter 3, have been directly manipulated to yield the passing rate desired by the commissioner of education. In general, in the early years, the cut scores are set high so as to yield a low passing rate and then adjusted downward to increase the passing rate. As I will document, low passing rates are then used to claim that the schools are failing and, therefore, the reform agenda of standardized tests and curriculum, or privatization, are necessary to improve education. For example, the low passing rate on the now annual Common Core State exams have been used by charter school CEOs to argue for more charter schools and by Governor Cuomo to argue for increasing the number and funding of charter schools.

Later, the cut scores are adjusted to yield increasing passing rates, which are then used to assert that the reforms are working. Consequently, the corporate reformers use both low and high scores to argue for their reform agenda. However, I will argue and provide evidence that scores on New York's tests are completely unreliable and inadmissible as evidence regarding the quality of the schools.

The Neoliberal Attack on Public Schools, Teachers, and Parents

The last 15 years of reforms in the New York public schools reflect the neoliberal agenda of privatization; the shift in control from the local to the state, federal, and national; and governance through standardized testing and other objective, quantifiable measures. In chapters 3 through 5 I will provide an in-depth analysis of the education reform efforts of Governor Cuomo, President Obama, the Bill and Melinda Gates Foundation, and Pearson. Here I will describe their relevance to my overall argument.

Over his first term as governor and now into his second term, Cuomo has increased his criticism of public schools and his support for charters and private religious and nonreligious schools. He has also received increased campaign donations from those who profit from legislation favoring charter and other private schools. According to a recent report, he has received $4.8 million over the last few years (Gonzalez, 2015a).

Early in his second term, Cuomo increased his attack on public schools and public school teachers. Cuomo vowed to break "one of the only remaining public monopolies"—public schools—by increasing the number of and funding for charter schools and providing significant tax credits for those donating to charter, parochial, and private schools. He describes the public schools as failing and "believe[s] [that] these kinds of changes [i.e. privatization] are probably the single best thing that [he] can do as governor that's going to matter long-term" (Lovett, 2014).

He also believes that test-score data will provide "real performance measures with some competition, which is why I like charter schools (sic)." Cuomo will push a plan that includes more incentives and sanctions, including basing 50% of a teacher's evaluation on students' scores on the state-funded but Pearson-produced standardized tests and another 35% based on teacher observations conducted by the state. He claims that this will "make it a more rigorous evaluation system" (Lovett, 2014).

Cuomo demeans teachers' and parents' motives by stating that he realizes "the teachers don't want to do the evaluations and they don't want to do rigorous evaluation," adding, "I get they [teachers] will be using it [resisting Cuomo's reform agenda] the way they used it, I believe—to get the parents upset last year about this entire Common Core agenda" (Lovett, 2014). He blames teachers for fomenting the determined community resistance to the CCSS in the spring of 2014 when thousands of parents spoke up at public hearings on the Common Core exams. For example, 700 people, mostly parents, filled a Rochester area high school auditorium on a weekday afternoon to protest the flawed standards, curriculum, and exams. Of the hundreds who waited in line, most for hours, for their two minutes to speak, only one—a local school superintendent—spoke in favor of the CCSS. In 2014, 60,000 parents boycotted New York's standardized exams in 2014, and the goal is to have 250,000 parents boycott the 2015 exams (NYSAPE, 2015). Cuomo either cannot imagine or assumes that there is political advantage in describing teachers and parents as incapable of thinking on their own and developing their own rationales.

Cuomo aims to break teaching as a profession by making it much more difficult for teachers to receive satisfactory ratings and to achieve tenure. The current system uses students' scores on standardized tests for 40% of the evaluation (Hursh, 2014). But Cuomo argues that because on the first round of the Common Core state exams only slightly more than 30% of the students were rated "proficient" (although the passing rate was predetermined by the commissioner), too many teachers received passing ratings. He refers to the teacher evaluation system as "baloney," ignoring that he took part in creating the system and, when it was implemented, referred to it as "one of the toughest in the country . . . ground-breaking . . . and exactly what is needed to transform schools" (Strauss, 2015).

Now, Cuomo proposes basing 50% of teachers' evaluations on their students or, in the case of teachers whose students do not take a standardized exam, other teachers' students or an assessment of the Standards of Learning. Cuomo wants the other 50% based on two observations with one conducted by "a so-called 'independent observer'—principal or administrator from outside or within the district, a SUNY/CUNY professor or a trained independent evaluator from a State Education Department list" (Saunders, 2015, p. 8).

Furthermore, Cuomo aims to substantially increase the percentage of teachers who will be found to be either "developing" or "ineffective." What number will ultimately satisfy him is not known. Moreover, he proposes making earning tenure almost impossible by requiring teachers to earn ratings of "effective" or "very effective" for five consecutive years before becoming eligible. If they fail to achieve those ratings for any single year, their tenure clock is reset. Cuomo's proposals were passed with slight modifications by the legislature, which I will describe later.

Karen Magee, the president of New York State United Teachers, summarizes that Cuomo:

> Proposes drastic, punitive and unsupportive changes in teacher evaluations and discipline, changes that essentially would gut tenure. He wants to double down on the misuse of high-stakes tests; proposes eviscerating collective bargaining over evaluations; offers a back-door voucher scheme that would provide tax credits to the wealthy patrons of charter schools; and wants state control over "failing schools," which would allow him to silence the voice of parents and eliminate collective bargaining agreements.
>
> And, although inequality in school funding has reached record levels on his watch—and half the state's school districts have less state aid today than in 2008—Cuomo would provide only about half the aid we need, while tying even that woefully inadequate amount to enacting his corporate hedge-funded "reform" agenda.
>
> (Magee, 2015, p. 50)

Cuomo's actions have the potential of ending teaching as a profession. In only a very small percentage of charter schools are the teachers unionized. Under state law, charter schools can avoid unionization if they initially open with fewer than 250 students. Charter schools, which often start with only a few grades and then add additional grades each year, almost always open with no more than 249 students. Because they are not unionized, teachers typically have no contracts and are hired and fired at will. They also do not typically have pension plans as they would in the public schools. There is, understandably, high teacher turnover (Ravitch, 2014).

Cuomo's proposals regarding teacher tenure, which were approved by the legislature with slight modifications, are intended to make achieving tenure almost impossible. Consequently, public school teaching is likely to follow the model provided by Teach for America: teaching will be perceived as a one- to three-year position undertaken before moving on to a career in a better paying and more respected field. Some have referred to this as the McDonaldization of the teaching profession.

Lastly, New York's public schools have been underfunded since the recession of 2008 while having to take on underfunded mandates such as RTTT Marcou-O'Malley, M. (2014) Moreover, the state has never complied with a court order to increase the funding for underfunded urban schools. In response, Cuomo offers a minimal increase in state funding unless the legislature passes into law all of his education reform proposals. Cuomo has made clear that he aims to portray public schools as failing, replace public schools with charter schools, and severely cripple if not destroy teachers' unions.

As disturbing as Cuomo's attack on teachers is, almost as disturbing is that he was the nominee of the more culturally liberal Democratic Party and that he, along with fellow Democrats Arne Duncan and Chicago's Mayor Rahm Emanuel (Nichols, 2015), has attacked public schools and teachers to a degree not previously seen in Democratic candidates. However, as I will show, candidates from both parties have adopted the neoliberal agenda. Both Democrats and Republicans are supporting privatization and are willing to take funds from wealthy hedge fund managers and neoliberal foundations. Cuomo epitomizes the degree to which such corporate policies have come to dominate education in the United States. It also shows how some politicians who take a progressive position on culture—Cuomo has promoted gay marriage and gun control and opposed hydrofracking—can take a neoliberal position on education.

In New York, Cuomo's neoliberal views on education fit in with others who have the power to decide education policy. For example, for the last several decades, the Democrats, who are the majority party in the state legislature and, therefore, have the power to appoint the members of the Board of Regents, have selected members who, in general, support neoliberal polices of high-states testing and privatization. In turn, the regents choose the chancellor to represent them and the commissioner of education to carry out their directives. Over the past decade, and most significantly during the implementation of RTTT and Cuomo's attack on teachers and push to increase the number and funding of charter schools, the governor, commissioner, and chancellor have supported one another (Hursh, 2014).

John King, who was commissioner during the bungled implementation of the CCSS and the recipient of most of the parents' and teacher's wrath, recently resigned as commissioner to become special assistant to Arne Duncan. Before departing, he and Chancellor Tisch worked closely with Cuomo to develop an aggressive agenda to toughen the teacher and school evaluations (Tisch & Berlin, 2014; Malatras, 2014). His replacement and now the interim commissioner recently coauthored with Chancellor Meryl Tisch (Tisch & Berlin, 2014) a letter to the governor reiterating their support of the governor's education initiatives, including their support for mayoral control, raising the cap on charter schools, "increasing the rigor of certification examinations for teachers and school building leaders," and creating a new evaluation system that "will achieve better differentiation" (p. 1) so that fewer teachers will receive high scores and more will receive low scores.

Not only are Cuomo's views not substantially different from the regents; they also are intertwined with and complement those of the Obama administration. Obama, like Cuomo, has been a liberal on most social issues. Moreover, like Cuomo, he and his secretary of education, Arne Duncan, have been critical of teachers and unions to a degree formerly unheard of among Democrats. Obama's RTTT initiative promotes converting more public schools to charter schools; adopting the Common Core standards and curriculum; and using standardized tests based on the Common Core to evaluate students, teachers, and schools. Such policies highlight the magnitude of the shift in the educational agenda. Democrats, Republicans, and the corporate and philanthropic elite seem to be unified in their critique of the current education system and teachers and the reforms that are, therefore, required. In the next chapter, I examine how it is that the neoliberal education reform policies have come to dominance.

References

AFT. (n.d.). History. *American Federation of Teachers*. Retrieved from http://www.aft.org/about/history

Atlanta Public Schools. (2015, February 2). Charter system application and cluster planning update. Retrieved from http://www.boarddocs.com/ga/aps/Board.nsf/files/9TAF987CBC45/$file/Charter%20System%20and%20Cluster%20Planning%20Update_February%20Board%20v2.pdf

Ball, S.J. (2012). *Global Education, Inc.: New Policy Networks and the Neoliberal Imaginary*. New York: Routledge.

Ball, S. J. (2015). Education, governance and the tyranny of numbers. *Journal of Education Policy, 30*(3), 299–301. http://dx.doi.org/10.1080/02680939.2015.1013271

Beadie, N. (1999). From student markets to credential markets: The creation of the Regents examination system in New York State, 1864–1890. *History of Education Quarterly, 39*(1): 1–30.

Block, F. & Somers, M. (2014). *The Power of Market Fundamentalism*. Cambridge, MA: Harvard University Press.

Bloomberg, M. (2015). Mike Bloomberg Entrepreneur website. Retrieved from http://www.mikebloomberg.com/index.cfm?objectid=87360FFB-C29C-7CA2-F92DC3FBE4A49054

Bracey, G.W. (2002, October). The 12th Bracey report on the condition of public education. *Phi Delta Kappan, 84*(2), 135–150.

Brooks, D. (2014, April 17). When the circus descends. *The New York Times*, A23.

Buras, K.L. (2014, December 26). Charter schools flood New Orleans. *The Progressive*. Retrieved from http://www.progressive.org/news/2014/12/187949/charter-schools-flood-new-orleans

Buras, K.L. (2015). *Charter Schools, Race, and Urban Space: Where the Market Meets Grassroots Resistance*. New York: Routledge.

Campbell, J. (2015, March 5). Pro-charter school rally packs Capital's lawn. *Democrat and Chronicle*, 8A.

Cassidy, J. (2015, January 5). What is Mario Cuomo's legacy? *The New Yorker 90*(42). Retrieved from http://www.newyorker.com/news/john-cassidy/mario-cuomos-legacy

Children's Defense Fund (2014). The state of America's children. Washington, D.C: Children's Defense Fund. Retrieved from: http://www.childrensdefense.org/library/state-of-americas-children/2014-soac.pdf?utm_source=2014-SOAC-PDF&utm_medium=link&utm_campaign=2014-SOAC

Chistianakis, M. & Mora, R. (2015). Charter schools and the privatization of public schools. In P. R. Carr & B.J. Porfilio (Eds.), *The Phenomenon of Obama and the Agenda for Education: Can Hope (Still) Audaciously Trump Neoliberalism?* (2nd ed.), 95–116. Charlotte, NC: Information Age Publishing.

Civil Rights Project (2014). New York's extreme school segregation: Inequality, inaction and a damaged future. Rochester, NY factsheet. Retrieved from http://civilrightsproject.ucla.edu/research/k-12-education/integration-and-diversity/ny-norflet-report-placeholder/Rochester_NY_CBSA_intrastate_tables_2014_March20_v.pdf

Confessore, N. (2015, January 26). Koch brothers' budget of $889 million is on par with both parties' spending. *The New York Times*, A1. Retrieved from http://www.nytimes.com/2015/01/27/us/politics/kochs-plan-to-spend-900-million-on-2016-campaign.html

Crouch, C. (2011). *The Strange Non-Death of Neoliberalism*. Malden, MA: Polity Press.

Darling-Hammond, L. (2014, June 27). *U.S. Release of the Teaching and Learning International Survey*. Stanford, CA: Stanford Center for Opportunity Policy in Education. Retrieved from https://edpolicy.stanford.edu/sites/default/files/events/materials/ppt-darling-hammond-talis.pdf

Dolan, K.A. & Kroll, L. (2015, March 2). Inside the 2015 Forbes billionaires list: Facts and figures. *Forbes*. Retrieved from http://www.forbes.com/sites/kerryadolan/2015/03/02/inside-the-2015-forbes-billionaires-list-facts-and-figures/

Egan, R. (1996). *Buying a Movement: Right-Wing Foundations and American Politics*. Washington, DC: People for the American Way Foundation. Retrieved from http://www.pfaw.org/pfaw/general/default.aspx?oid=2052 and can be downloaded in PDF format at http://www.pfaw.org/sites/default/files/buyingamovement.pdf

Foucault, M. (1979). *Discipline and Punish*. Hammondsworth: Penguin.

The Foundation Center. Foundation Stats. HYPERLINK "http://data.foundationcenter.org/" \l "/fc1000/subject:all/all/top:foundations/list/2012" http://data.foundationcenter.org/#/fc1000/subject:all/all/top:foundations/list/2012. P. 1

Gates, B. (2009, January). 2009 Annual letter from Bill Gates. Retrieved from http://www.gatesfoundation.org/who-we-are/resources-and-media/annual-letters-list/annual-letter-2009

Giroux, H. (2012, June 19). Beyond the politics of the big lie: The education deficit and the new authoritarianism. *Truthout*. http://www.truth-out.org/opinion/item/9865

Gonzalez, J. (2015, March 11). Hedge fund executives give 'til it hurts to politicians, especially Cuomo, to get more chart schools. *New York Daily News*. Retrieved from http://www.nydailynews.com/new-york/education/hedge-fund-execs-money-charter-schools-pay-article-1.2145001

Hanson, F.A. (1993). *Testing, Testing: Social Consequences of the Examined Life*. Berkeley: University of California Press.

Harvey, D. (2005). *A Brief History of Neoliberalism*. Oxford: Oxford University Press.

Hassard, J. (2014, March 15). Why Bill Gates defends the Common Core. *The Art of Teaching Science*. Retrieved from http://www.artofteachingscience.org/why-bill-gates-defends-the-common-core/

Hayek, F.A. (1944). *The Road to Serfdom*. Chicago: University of Chicago Press.

Hursh, D. (2008). *High-Stakes Testing and the Decline of Teaching and Learning*. Lanham, MD: Rowman & Littlefield.

Hursh, D. (2014, November 1). *Why Economic Theory Matters: How Neoliberalism Purposely Undermines Our Ability to Make Sense of our Current Crises*. American Educational Studies Association annual conference. Toronto, Canada.

Hursh, D. (2015). Even more of the same: How free market education dominates education. In *The Phenomenon of Obama and the Agenda for Education: Can Hope Audaciously Trump Neoliberalism?* Charlotte, NC: Information Age Press.

Integrated Postsecondary Education Data System (2014). Retrieved from http://nces.ed.gov/collegenavigator/?s=NY&zc=14627&zd=0&of=3

Johnson, D. C. & Salle, L. M. (2004, November). *Responding to the Attack on Public Education and Teacher Unions: A Commonweal Institute Report*. Menlo Park: CA, Commonweal Institute. Retrieved November 25, 2004, from http://www.commonwealinstitute.org/IssuesEducation.htm

Kahlenberg, R. & Potter. H. (2014–2015). Restoring Shanker's Vision for Charter Schools. *American Educator, 38*(4), 4–13.

Kovacs, P.E. (Ed.). (2011). *The Gates Foundation and the Future of U.S. "Public" Schools*. New York: Routledge.

Kruse, K. M. (2015). *One Nation under God: How Corporate America Invented Christian America*. New York: Perseus Books Group.

Kucsera, J. (2014, March 26). New York State's extreme school segregation: Inequality, inaction and a damaged future. Los Angeles. *The Civil Rights Project of UCLA*. Retrieved from http://civilrightsproject.ucla.edu/research/k-12-education/integration-and-diversity/ny-norflet-report-placeholder

Ladd, C. (2015, April 30). A chance to end the public school era. *Chron (Houston Chronicle)* on-line. Retrieved from http://blog.chron.com/goplifer/2015/04/a-chance-to-end-the-public-school-era/

Leonardatos, H. & Zahedi, K. (2014, September). Accoutability and "racing to the top" in New York State: A report from the frontlines. *Teachers College Record 116*(9), 1–23.

Lovett, K. (2014, October 27). Cuomo will push new teacher evaluations, vows to bust school "monopoly" if elected. *New York Daily News*. Retrieved from http://www.nydailynews.com/news/politics/cuomo-vows-bust-school-monopoly-re-elected-article-1.1989478

Magee, K.E. (2015, February). Beating the billionaires' agenda. *NYSUT United, 5*(3), 5.

Malatras, J. (2014, December 18). Letter to Chancellor Tisch and Commissioner King from Jim Malatras, Director of State Operations.

Marcou-O'Malley, M. (2014). Billions behind: New York State continues to violate Students' constitutional rights. New York: Alliance for Quality Education. http://www.aqeny.org/wp-content/uploads/2014/08/REPORT-NY-Billions-Behind.pdf

Natriello, G. & Pallas, A. M. (1999). The development and impact of high stakes testing. *ERIC*. ED443871.

New York State Allies for Public Education (2015, January 21). NYS Parents fight to reclaim student education from excessive testing and data collection: 250,000 high-stakes test boycotts planned statewide. Retrieved from http://www.nysape.org/250000-high-stakes-test-boycotts-planned-statewide-nys-parents-fight-to-reclaim-student-education-from-excessive-testing-and-data-collection.html

Nichols, J. (2015, February 25). Rahm Emanuel seemed unstoppable—until he ticked off Chicago's teachers. *The Nation*. Retrieved from http://www.thenation.com/blog/199097/how-fight-over-public-education-just-disrupted-politics-chicago

Olssen, M., Codd, J. & O'Neill, A-M. (2004). *Education Policy: Globalization, Citizenship, and Democracy*. Thousand Oaks, CA: Sage.

Peck, J. (2010). *Constructions of Neoliberalism*. Oxford: Oxford University Press.

Pedroni, T. (2011). Urban shrinkage as a performance of whiteness: neoliberal urban restructuring, education, and racial containment in the post-industrial, global niche city. *Discourse: Studies in the Cultural Politics of Education, 32*(2), 203–215.

Pickett, K. & Wilkinson, R. (2011). *The Spirit Level: Why Greater Equality Makes Societies Stronger*. New York: Bloomsbury Press.

Powell, L. (1971, August 23). *The Powell Memo*. Retrieved from http://reclaimdemocracy.org/powell_memo_lewis/

Ravitch, D. (2013). *Reign of Error: The Hoax of the Privatization Movement and the Danger to America's Public Schools*. New York: Knopf.

Ravitch, D. (2014, September 24). The secret to Eva Moskowitz' "success." *The Nation*. Retrieved from http://www.thenation.com/article/181752/secret-eva-moskowitzs-success#

Rich, M. (2015, January 16). Percentage of poor student in public schools rises. *The New York Times*. Retrieved from http://www.nytimes.com/2015/01/17/us/school-poverty-study-southern-education-foundation.html

Sachs, J. (2014, November 6). Understanding and overcoming America's plutocracy. *Huffington Post*. Retrieved from http://www.huffingtonpost.com/jeffrey-sachs/understanding-and-overcom_b_6113618.html

Sachs, J. (2015, March 10). By separating nature from economics, we have walked blindly into tragedy. *The Guardian*. Retrieved from http://www.theguardian.com/global-development-professionals-network/2015/mar/10/jeffrey-sachs-economic-policy-climate-change

Saltman, K.J. (2010). *The Gift of Education: Public Education and Venture Philanthropy*. New York: Palgrave.

Saunders, S. (2015, February). NYSUT blisters Cuomo's draconian anti-teacher agenda. *NYSUT United*. Lathnam: New York State United Teachers.

Schneider, M.K. (2013, August 27). A brief audit of Bill Gate's Common Core spending. Retrieved from https://deutsch29.wordpress.com/2013/08/27/a-brief-audit-of-bill-gates-common-core-spending/

Schneider, M. K. (2014a, March 17). Gates dined on March 13, 2014 with 80 Senators. Retrieved from https://deutsch29.wordpress.com/2014/03/17/gates-dined-on-march-13-2014-with-80-senators/

Schneider, M. K. (2014b, November 23). Obama's USDOE: Appointed to Privatize. Period. Retrieved from https://deutsch29.wordpress.com/2014/11/23/obamas-usdoe-appointed-to-privatize-period/

Sharp, B. (2014, September 19). Over 50% of Rochester's kids live in poverty. *Democrat and Chronicle*. Retrieved from http://www.democratandchronicle.com/story/news/2014/09/18/rochesters-children-live-poverty/15856493/

Simmonds, M. & Webb, P.T. (2013). Accountability synopticism: How a think tank and the media developed a quasi-market for school choice in British Columbia. *The International Education Journal: Comparative Perspectives, 12*(2), 21–41.

Southern Education Foundation. (2014). A New Majority Research Bulletin: Low Income Students Now a Majority in the Nation's Public Schools. Atlanta, Georgia: Southern Education Foundation. Retrieved from http://www.southerneducation. org/Our-Strategies/Research-and-Publications/New-Majority-Diverse-Majority-Report-Series/A-New-Majority-2015-Update-Low-Income-Students-No

Strauss, V. (2014a, January 18). Everything you needed to know about Common Core-Ravitch. *The Washington Post.* Retrieved from http://www.washingtonpost.com/blogs/answer-sheet/wp/2014/01/18/everything-you-need-to-know-about-common-core-ravitch/

Strauss. V. (2014b, December 10). Obama's Race to the Top loses all funding in 2015 omnibus spending bill. *The Washington Post.* Retrieved from http://www.washingtonpost.com/blogs/answer-sheet/wp/2014/12/10/obamas-race-to-the-top-loses-all-funding-in-2015-omnibus-spending-bill/

Strauss, V. (2015, January 1). Teacher evaluation: Going from bad to worse? *The Washington Post.* Retrieved from http://www.washingtonpost.com/blogs/answer-sheet/wp/2015/01/01/teacher-evaluation-going-from-bad-to-worse/

Taylor, K. (2015, April 6). At Success Academy charter schools, high scores and polarizing tactics. *The New York Times,* A-1. Retrieved from http://www.nytimes.com/2015/04/07/nyregion/at-success-academy-charter-schools-polarizing-methods-and-superior-results.html?emc=edit_na_20150406&nlid=15744368&_r=1

Tisch, M.H. & Berlin, E.R. (2014, December 31). Tisch and Berlin letter to Jim Maltras, Director of State Operations, State of New York, Executive Chamber, Albany, NY. Retrieved from http://www.p12.nysed.gov/docs/nysed-malatras-letter-12-31-14.pdf

Williams, R. (2013). Cost table of APPR in the district. Honeoye Falls-Lima School District, New York.

Winerip, M. (2011, December 19). 10 years of assessing students with scientific exactitude. *The New York Times,* A24.

Wohlstetter, P. & Houston, D.M. (2015, January 30). Rage against the regime: The reform of education policy in New York City. *Teachers College Record.* Retrieved from http://www.tcrecord.org/Content.asp?ContentID=17841

2

UNDERSTANDING THE RISE
OF NEOLIBERAL POLICIES

So far I have described some of the ways in which the neoliberal corporate reforms have transformed education, with their emphasis on high stakes standardized testing, privatization, and accountability, or what Ball (2015) describes as the "tyranny of numbers" (p. 299). In this chapter, I want to situate those reforms within six societal dynamics, all of which I have already alluded to but now want to investigate further. Moreover, identifying these dynamics will provide insights into what we might do to counter the corporate reform agenda and develop a social democratic alternative (Scheurich, 1994).

First, we face two conflicting social imaginaries: the social democratic imaginary prevailed in the United States from 1933 through about 1980, when neoliberalism became dominant. Rolling back neoliberalism will require developing a new conception that builds on past social democratic ideals but incorporates new ways of thinking about the relationship between one another and to the environment (Henderson & Hursh, 2014).

Second, economic and political power have been concentrated in the hands of the rich, who are unelected and unaccountable and gain influence through means outside the democratic process. Therefore, as I will describe, we need to develop forms of governance that are more transparent and promote democratic decision making.

Third, corporate reformers focus on education as a means of reducing economic inequality to avoid confronting the inequalities created by neoliberal capitalism. Pushing back will require both promoting more democratic forms of education and also working to reduce economic inequality and poverty and provide health care, housing, and other services that improve the quality of life.

Fourth, the rise of neoliberalism parallels the change from government to governance that includes replacing bureaucratic managerialism with new public management that emphasizes efficiency, measurement, and data. While we now have the technology to create all kinds of data, data remains limited in what it can tell us about how teachers teach and students learn, as well as the relations between teachers and students in the classroom.

Fifth, the rise of networks and change in scales within new public management governance has transformed how power is accessed. Ball (2012) describes the rise of networks as a substantial change in governance that represents the "institutionalization of power relations (Marsh & Smith, 2000, p. 6)" (p. 10). He further describes how networks enable governments to bring in the public, private, and voluntary sectors to solve their community's problems and constitute a new form of governance in which "the boundaries between state, economy, and civil society are being blurred," (p. 7) permitting new voices in the policy conversations. However, because the rise of networks is accompanied by a shift in scales, with decisions made increasingly at the federal, national, and international scales, these new voices are not likely to be citizens or groups of citizens but those who already have the connections that make taking advantage of the network possible. Instead, we can work to make network governance transparent and design ways to include those both historically and recently excluded.

Finally, market fundamentalists promote the idea that societal and economic decisions should be made through markets, rather than the political process. In response, I concur with Block and Somers (2014) that all decisions are really political decisions. They write that, "the project of creating self-regulating markets is ultimately impossible" and "has never—and cannot ever—actually exist." They have examined how "markets are always organized through politics and social practices" (p. 10) and what this means for contemporary debate. Most importantly, they argue, market fundamentalists are not setting "the market free from the state but [are] instead *re-embedding* it in *different* political, legal, and cultural arrangements, ones that mostly disadvantage the poor and the middle class, and advantage wealth and corporate interests" (p. 9, italics in original). In fact, recognizing that neoliberalism is necessarily political and that it privileges some groups over others helps refute the notion that we can and should use markets to make all decisions.

By articulating that there exist different conceptions of these six social dynamics, and that some reflect market fundamentalist and neoliberal conceptions and some social democratic, we can begin to articulate alternatives to the current dominate conceptions. In critiquing the neoliberal conceptions, I am not aiming to return to the social democratic conceptions that dominated pre-1980. Rather, I want to suggest ways that we might respond to the changing technologies and our environmental and political crises.

Neoliberals Have Gained Control over the Dominant Social Imaginary

In this section, I argue that the current corporate education reform movement has replaced the once dominant social democratic social imaginary that emphasized collective action, community, trust, and common purpose (Judt, 2010) with neo-liberal conceptions emphasizing free markets, individual choice, and competition. They have succeeded, in part, by making the following argument: that economic growth requires an economic system in which corporations are free to innovate within a market system. Furthermore, a growing economy requires skilled, efficient workers produced by teachers and schools that are held accountable.

In addition, our schools, corporate reformers claim, are performing more poorly and inequality and poverty have increased because, under social demo-cratic liberalism, the state (government) failed to demand accountability and per-mitted the schools and society as a whole to fall behind those of other countries. In response, claim the corporate reformers, the education system needs to be reformed by creating charter schools that would compete with the publicly man-aged schools and by holding students, teachers, and schools accountable through standardized testing. Consequently, because standardized testing and school priva-tization will, goes the argument, result in improved schools for all, testing and privatization are part of the new civil rights movement.

Therefore, I will begin by defining the concept of social imaginary and argu-ing that over the last 45 years the once dominant social democratic social imagi-nary has been largely, but not entirely, replaced by the neoliberal social imaginary. I will then briefly describe the rise of neoliberalism in education policy and how it has been promoted by both raising false fears over the state of education and describing reforms that are based on privatization and competition as socially just.

The neoliberal/market fundamentalist social imaginary diametrically differs from that based on the social democratic principles that prevailed from the mid-1930s to the early 1970s. Which notion attains dominance is crucial because as Taylor (2004), who first described the notion of social imaginary, writes, "the social imaginary is the way in which people imagine their social existence, how they fit together with others, how things go between them and their fellows . . . the expectations that are normally met, and the deeper normative notions and images that underlie these expectations" (p. 23).

The notion of the social imaginary is useful because it suggests that societies as a whole adopt a particular way of looking at the world, ways that limit their vision in terms of what is possible. Rizvi and Lingard (2010) state that:

> A social imaginary is a way of thinking shared in a society by ordinary people. The common understandings that make everyday practices pos-sible, giving them sense and legitimacy. It is largely implicit, embedded in ideas and practices, carrying within it deeper normative notions and images, constitutive of society.
>
> (p. 34)

Social imaginaries differ from social theory in that they are held by large groups of people and often communicated in stories and anecdotes. However, while they may be less theoretical, they are no less powerful because they shape how people think about the role of government and the "nature and scope of political authority" (Rizvi & Lingard, p. 13). The notion of social imaginary reminds us that how people view the world is largely contested, not theoretically but at the level of lived experience. Consequently, we, as scholars and members of the educational community, must explicitly engage in problematizing social imaginaries.

As I described earlier, the dominant social imaginary from the mid-1930s to the early 1970s was social democratic liberalism. However, it was not uncontested. Beginning in the 1940s, neoliberal economic and political theories became increasingly part of the conversation with the publication of Hayek's *The Road to Serfdom* (1944). University of Chicago economist Milton Friedman's publication (1952, 1962) was the leading promoter of neoliberalism in the United States, and his writing was published in popular publications such as *Readers Digest*, *Saturday Evening Post*, and *Newsweek* (Ebenstein, 2007).

Kruse (2015) describes how conservative Christian churches and organizations worked together with the Chamber of Commerce and other neoliberal business organizations to push back against the welfare state and governmental limits on corporations. Similarly, Fones-Wolf, in *Selling Free Enterprise: The Business Assault on Labor and Liberalism* (1994), describes how corporate leaders desired that schools socialize workers for the factory and promote social and political stability.

However, neoliberalism only became dominant in the United States in the 1970s after the circulation of the Powell memo (1971) that articulated the dangers capitalism faced from the social democratic forces promoting economic, gender, and racial equality. Neoliberals and neoconservatives responded to Powell's memo by creating and funding dozens of organizations, including the Heritage Foundation, the Hoover Institution, the American Enterprise Institute, and the American Legislative Exchange Council (ALEC) (Block & Somers, 2014; Harvey, 2005, pp. 43–44).

Finally, in 1975, neoliberals had a chance to put the theories into practice when the United States assisted in overthrowing the elected socialist Chilean government of Salvador Allende and replacing him with the dictator Augusto Pinochet. Pinochet's chief economic advisors were trained by Milton Friedman at the University of Chicago (dubbed "the Chicago Boys") and advised Pinochet on reducing the role of the state and increasing privatization and marketization (Peck, 2010).

Neoliberalism came to full fruition in the 1980s in the United States under President Reagan and in the United Kingdom under Prime Minister Margaret Thatcher. Thatcher seems to actually have read Hayek, as she was once observed slamming down Hayek's *Constitution of Liberty* (1960) on a table while declaring "*This* is what I believe" (Ranelagh, 1992; cited in Peck, italics added, 2010, p. xv).

Thatcher aimed to crush unions and any other resistance to her policies of privatizing public enterprises, such as public housing and the railroads, and dismantling or rolling back commitments to the welfare state, while creating a favorable business climate. During the miners' strike of 1984–85, she used "police and security services to infiltrate and undermine the miners' union," going so far as to brand workers as "enemies of democracy" and to treat them as outlaws (Milne, 2014).

Reagan reduced public spending, attacked and dismantled unions such as the air traffic controllers union (PATCO), and deregulated numerous industries including airlines and communication (Harvey, 2005, pp. 23–27). Together, Thatcher, Reagan, and their corporate supporters aimed to restore the corporate profits that had slumped during the recession though neoliberal policies emphasizing "the deregulation of the economy, trade liberalization, the dismantling of the public sector [such as education, health, and social welfare], and the predominance of the financial sector of the economy over production and commerce" (Vilas, 1996, p. 16).

Since the 1980s, neoliberalism has become the dominant social imaginary, as shrinking the size of the government and creating competitive free markets has become so natural as to be unquestioned. Francis Fukuyama, in his 1992 book *The End of History*, declared that with the fall of the Berlin Wall, free market capitalism had won and other alternatives had lost. Thomas Friedman, the *New York Times* columnist and best-selling author of *The World Is Flat: A Brief History of the Twenty-first Century* (2005) and *The Lexus and the Olive Tree* (1999), describes free market capitalism as both desirable and inevitable. He wrote:

> The driving force behind globalization is free market capitalism—the more you let market forces rule and the more you open your economy to free trade and competition, the more efficient your economy will be. Globalization means the spread of free-market capitalism to virtually every country in the world. Therefore, globalization also has its own set of economic rules—rules that revolve around opening, deregulating and privatizing your economy, in order to make it more competitive and attractive to foreign investment.
>
> (Friedman, p. 119)

In education, neoliberal policies echo both Friedman's economic and political goals of creating markets, efficiency, privatizing services including schools, and expanding the economy. Consequently, schools are to focus on efficiency and producing graduates who are "college and career ready."

I do not want to pretend that all is well with the public schools; in fact, I have argued throughout my 45-year career as an educator that students in the United States receive an unequal education based on race, class, gender, and (dis)ability and that the dominant curriculum and pedagogy is inadequate in teaching students to raise questions and solve problems. I have not argued for more testing or that schools should be privatized. Rather, I have argued that students would learn more if they and their teachers were supported in their efforts and poverty and racial and economic segregation were decreased.

However, as Berliner and Biddle (1995) demonstrated 20 years ago and Berliner (2014) last year, critics of public education have created "manufactured crises" to describe the schools as failing and, therefore, requiring rigorous standardized assessments and privatization. The rise of neoliberalism in the United States was accompanied by increasing attacks on public education, beginning with the 1983 report from the National Commission on Excellence in Education (NCEE) that declared that we were "a nation at risk." The NCEE claimed, without providing evidence, that the average achievement of high school students on most standardized tests is now lower that 26 years ago when Sputnik was launched (1983, p. 8) and such a "rising tide of mediocrity" was eroding "the educational foundations of our society" that "threatened our very future as a Nation and a people" (p. 5).

Since then, as many have pointed out (Hursh, 2008), critics have repeatedly warned us that the United States is in danger of losing to other countries, particularly when the scores on the Programme for International Student Assessment (PISA) scores are made public. As just one of many examples, *Rising Above the Gathering Storm: Energizing and Employing America for a Brighter Future*, written by the Committee on Prospering in the Global Economy of the 21st Century by the prestigious National Academy of Sciences (2007), warns that the United States is losing in the global competition because our schools are inadequate.

While the debate over the educational purposes of education has raged since the turn of the previous century with two contrasting aims: improving economic efficiency and competitiveness (Snedden, 1915, 1924; Yerkes, 1919) versus Dewey's (1915, 1938/1963) notion of preparing students as democratic citizens, the debate, I would argue, this time is different. The corporate reformers have succeeded in transforming the dominant social imaginary and, as I will argue in more depth in the next chapter, reorganizing schools so that it is much harder to undo the reforms.

The corporate reform agenda has not only been promoted on the grounds of economic efficiency; the reformers have also largely captured the discourse regarding civil rights. Supporters of standardized exams, charter schools, and choice have argued that choice is a civil right and that these corporate reforms continue the legacy begun by Martin Luther King, Jr. and the civil rights movement. Even though charter schools do not have to serve children with disabilities or who are English language learners, and can and do expel students at a much higher rate than public schools, and undermine students' right to an education managed by the public and not a private corporation, charter school supporters argue that they, not supporters of desegregation or fair and equitable funding, are the real supporters of civil rights.

That neoliberalism has gained dominance is reflected, as I will show, in the way that we discuss education and its relationship to society. Neoliberals dismiss arguments that something should be done about the increasing inequality and poverty in society, stating that "all children can learn" and that those who raise the issue of poverty are not willing to institute the desired corporate education reforms that will enable all children to learn. Similarly, Governor Cuomo declares that restoring school funding to the levels before the recession of 2008 and in response to increasing levels of family and child poverty perpetuates the misguided idea that problems can be solved "by throwing money at them" McKinley, J. (2015, March 10). Instead, holding students and teachers accountable through scores on standardized tests and privatizing education is the solution.

For example, Cuomo and the previous mayor of New York City, Michael Bloomberg, both have positioned teachers as "special interests," only interested in their own careers. At the same time, they have promoted their agenda of mayoral control of schools, and holding students and teachers accountable through high-stakes standardized testing, by invoking Martin Luther King, Jr. and the Civil Rights movement of the 1960s. Bloomberg and Cuomo used separate 2012 observances marking Dr. King's birthday to assail teachers as the primary cause for the failures of the city's educational system. Bloomberg, who has proposed that schools be improved by firing half the teachers and doubling salaries and class size (Strauss, 2011), declared that he is "ready to fight for the kids: I'm ready to stand up to special interests." Similarly, Cuomo advocated: "we have to realize that our schools are not an employment program. . . . It is this simple: It is not about the adults; it is about the children." Bloomberg and Cuomo portray themselves as defenders of the children's civil rights, citing the 1954 Brown v. Board of Education ruling. Governor Cuomo has lamented that because of failing schools, "the great equalizer that was supposed to be the public education system can now be the great discriminator" (Kaplan & Taylor, 2012, A-17).

In the spring of 2014, Cuomo led a rally at the state capitol promoting charter schools. At the rally he stated that, "education is not about the districts and not about the pensions and not about the unions and not about the lobbyists and not about the PR firms—education is about the students, and the students come first" (Cuomo, 2014). Similarly, when he proposed his education reforms, he stated, "let's remember the children in the process. And then we'll end up doing the right thing" (Blain & Lovett, 2015).

As I will expand upon later, Cuomo portrays himself as above the lobbyists, who he seems to imply are only educators, but not the hedge fund managers who have spent millions to fund his campaign and who have advised him on rewriting education policy (Teachout & Khan, 2014). For example, in the summer of 2014, he worked closely with Education Reform Now to organize a three-day retreat, "Camp Philos," on education reform at Whiteface Lodge in the Adirondacks.

As I will describe in more depth later, Education Reform Now is a nonprofit advocacy group that lobbies state and federal officials to support charter schools, evaluate teachers based on student test scores, and eliminate tenure for teachers (Ravitch, 2014c). However, teachers were explicitly excluded from the event.

Neoliberals Have Gained Sufficient Economic and Political Power to Control the Direction of Reform

In the previous section, I argued that corporate reformers have largely succeeded in replacing the previous social democratic social imaginary with a neoliberal one and suggested that they have accomplished this through different organizations that promote a neoliberal discourse and by situating a discourse of individualism and competition within the discourse of the civil rights movement. Here, I will briefly describe some of the motivations for their efforts, including profit, political power, and a desire to divert the public's attention from the more substantial and intractable issues of poverty, inequality, and inadequate housing and health care.

The corporate reformers recognize that there is a lot of money to be made in schools, especially by taking assessments and curriculum out of the hands of teachers in schools and centralizing them at the state level. Numerous research- ers have examined how education has been privatized in the interest of making a profit (Buras, 2015; Saltman, 2007). However, here and in the next chapters, I will focus only on two: Pearson Education, with Michael Barber as their chief education advisor, and Microsoft, which is not headed by Bill Gates, but, I would argue, through the Bill and Melinda Gates Foundation, engages in activities that will benefit Microsoft. For example, Pearson and Microsoft have a joint contract to develop the standardized tests and curriculum for New York State, which Gates wants delivered on Microsoft technology.

The educational involvement of both companies is too extensive to enu- merate, and I will only begin to enumerate here. Ball, in *Global Education Inc.: New Policy Networks and the Neo-liberal Imaginary* (2012), describes Pearson as the "world's largest education company with offices in thirty countries" (p. 124) aim- ing to "position itself as offering 'solutions' to the national policy problems of rais- ing standards and achieving educational improvements linked to both individual opportunity and national competitiveness" (p. 126). Pearson operates "across all three educational 'message systems'—pedagogy, curriculum, and assessment and joining these up, globally, across a range of media within its products and business growth plan" (p. 127).

In the United States, Simon (2015), in a report for *Politico*, states that Pearson:

> [W]rites the textbooks and tests that drive instruction in public schools
> across the nation. Its software grades student essays, tracks student behavior
> and diagnoses—and treats—attention deficit disorder. The company admin-
> isters teacher licensing exams and coaches teachers once they are in the

classroom. It advises principals. It operates a network of three dozen online public schools. It co-owns the for-profit company that now administers the GED. A top executive boasted in 2012 that Pearson is the largest custodian of student data anywhere.

(p. 4)

Moreover, Simon reports that Pearson's "globally adjusted profit for 2013 topped $1 billion" in North America (p. 7).

I have not seen a list for the standardized tests for which Pearson has contracts at the state level nor for countries other than the United States. Any list would be outdated as soon as it is compiled. Also, my lists for the United States and New York are likely to be incomplete. However, at the national level, Pearson develops and administers the National Assessment of Educational Progress (National Center for Educational Statistics, 2015), the Stanford Achievement Test, the Miller Analogy Test, and the Graduate Equivalency Test (GED). It was also recently awarded a major contract worth $63 million to develop the Partnership for Assessment of Readiness for College and Careers (PARCC) to assess whether students are on track for college (Delevingne, 2015). It also won the contract to design the Programme for International Student Assessment, or PISA exam, starting in 2015 (Ravitch, 2014b).

In New York, Pearson received $32.1 million over five years to create, administer, and grade the Common Core Exams in English language arts and math. Pearson has also received $108 million from New Jersey and $60 million from Maryland (Delevingne, 2015). It is also responsible for edTPA in New York and nationwide (www.edtpa.com). Pearson designs, administers, and grades the state's teacher certification exams, including the video and portfolio assessment of student teachers, for which students pay $300 per test.

Pearson Education also owns most of the major publishers of K–12 and higher education textbooks and trade books. Their imprints include: Adobe, Scott Foresman, Penguin, Longman, Wharton, Harcourt, Puffin, Prentice Hall, Allyn & Bacon, and Random House.

Pearson would not be benefitting from the Common Core requirements if it were not for Bill Gates. As described by Layton (2014), the Common Core was floundering until, in 2008, Gene Wilhoit, director of a national group of state school chiefs, and David Coleman, promoter of standards and now president and CEO of the College Board, met with Bill Gates to ask for his help pushing the CCSS forward. Gates has done more than help. As detailed later, he has invested at least $3.2 billion in promoting the Common Core, funding almost every organization whose support might conceivably help.

Gates has protested against those who see more than altruistic motives behind his funding of the Common Core, stating that as the world's wealthiest person, he hardly needs to be the technological solutions to the world's problems, including education but also health and agriculture (Hursh, 2011b). Moreover,

Microsoft, founded by Gates, has financial interests that complement Pearson's. As mentioned, the Common Core State Standards require that schools use computers to assess students. In February 2014, Gates announced that they were joining with Pearson to deliver the "Common Core classroom materials on Microsoft's tablet, the Surface" (Layton, 2014). Such a development has a huge benefit for Microsoft and anyone who holds Microsoft stock, such as Gates with $14 billion. One might think that Gates' fortune would be large enough, but then one could have thought that when it was half as large.

Just as importantly, the impact that the Bill and Melinda Gates Foundation has had on education policy reflects that change in the relationship between philanthropists and nonprofit institutions such as schools. While philanthropy has always had its political dimension (Barken, 2013), it has become much more so over the past few decades. The major education philanthropists, such as Bill and Melinda Gates, the Walton family (Walmart), Eli Broad, Laura and John Arnold, and Michael and Susan Dell, are not interested in donating money so that their name can adorn a building. Instead, they use their wealth to engage in what Saltman (2010, 2012) calls venture philanthropy. Venture philanthropists aim to use philanthropy to design and implement education policies reflecting their neoliberal political agenda of privatization, markets, efficiency, and accountability. As I will show, the foundations mentioned above use their wealth to actively promote their vision of society, including funding agencies to support and carry out their political goals. Barken (2013) describes other instances where the Gates Foundation created organizations to politically support their agenda, such as when they set up Communities for Teaching Excellence to support Teachers First.

Consequently, venture philanthropists significantly impact education policy in the United States, as Saltman (2010), Kovacs (2011), Buras (2014), and Lipman (2007) have described. In fact, Bill Gates, through his philanthropic investments, has, I will argue, a greater impact on education than any other single person or organization.

In addition, it is difficult to keep track of the funding that the Gates Foundation and other philanthropic organizations give to nongovernment organizations, universities, and other educational organizations. Instead of hierarchical systems, we now face heterarchical systems in which decisions are made at different places as part of a web of decision making.

Sometimes, the efforts of neoliberal foundations are not merely difficult to track but impossible because they are secret. In New York, the Gates and other neoliberal organizations have funded special secret advisors to Commissioner King. Only in spring 2013, after three years of operation, was it revealed that the commissioner hired 23 secret advisors, called the Regents Researchers, with expertise primarily in testing, who received annual salaries of over $200,000 each. The $16.5 million in funding for these advisors come from several philanthropic foundations, with, not surprisingly, the largest amount ($3 million) coming from the Bill and Melinda Gates Foundation. In addition, the Regent fellows received a founding gift from the James S. and (Chancellor) Merryl Tisch Fund, the Leona and Harry Helmsley Charity, and the GE Fund.

Commissioner King responded to critics who complained that his policy advisors were hired in secret and paid out of funds provided secretly by philanthropists such as Bill Gates by claiming that they only served as advisors and he was under no obligation to follow their advice. However, given the amount of funding, over $4 million per year, and the fact that one of the foundations was established by Chancellor Tisch, who is essentially King's employer, the incentive to follow their advice is substantial (Odato, 2013).

Subsequently, corporations and foundations have influence education policies in ways that most citizens, including educators, are unable to and to make a profit for their companies. Their interventions into education have the additional advantage of shifting our attention from where it should be: inequality and poverty (Berliner, 2013).

Education Reform Is a Purposeful Distraction from the Problems with Neoliberal Policies

Given that neoliberal philosophy subscribes to the notion that society should be governed by markets and that markets are self-regulating, neoliberals are loath to develop policies that counteract the "natural" outcome of the markets. Nor is it in the neoliberals' interests to do so as neoliberal policies in the United States have resulted in increased income for the wealthy and stagnant incomes for everyone else.

At a talk in Rochester, New York, in fall 2014, Ravitch (2014a) submitted that the focus on standards and charter schools by the Billionaires Boys Club is a "purposeful distraction" from paying attention to the more difficult social problems that will improve students' learning: eliminating poverty, ending hunger, providing health care, and creating for parents well-paying and meaningful jobs. Similarly, Apple has, for the last several decades, talked about how the corporate reform effort has been used to:

> [E]xport the blame for our economic and social tragedies onto schools, without providing sufficient support to do anything serious about these tragedies. And, finally, it will be used to justify curricula, pedagogic relations, and mechanism of evaluation that will be even less lively and more alienating than those that are in place now.
>
> (Apple, 1996b, p. 4)

Instead, neoliberals claim that corporate education reform is the appropriate remedy for inequality in society. David Brooks (2015), *New York Times* columnist, reflects a variant of this view in a recent column where he states that there is no need to consider ways to redistribute wealth in society. Rather, we just need to increase "worker productivity" through education. Moreover, he writes that "no redistributionist measure will have the same long-term effect as good early-childhood education and better community colleges" (p. A29), somehow forgetting that over the last 30 years worker productivity has increased by 240% while median income has remained flat (Gilson, 2011). Only the rich have gotten richer, while everyone else works harder for no financial gain.

Governments, notes Apple (1996a), in order to retain legitimacy, must be seen as doing something about inequality. Rather than intervening in the economic system to redistribute wealth, as Brooks (2015) fears above, the neoliberals engage in education reform. Apple (1996a) notes that "governments must be seen to be doing something. . . . Reforming education is not only widely acceptable and relatively unthreatening, but just as crucially, is success or failure will not be obvious in the short term" (p. 88). Proponents of charter schools and high-stakes testing claim that those reforms have a positive impact on education, while opponents claim the opposite. Lacking a resolution buys time to avoid tackling the larger social issues and to continue with reforms that benefit corporations and hedge-fund investors.

Furthermore, as we have seen, the test results are manipulated to rise and fall based on what suits the reformers. High failing rates, such as on the recent Common Core exams in New York, serve as a rationale for demanding more charter schools and regulations, making it harder for teachers to received satisfactory ratings or achieve tenure. At other times, higher passing rates are used to claim that the corporate reforms are succeeding.

In addition, what we have observed in New York is an increased attack not only on teachers but also on teachers' unions. As described earlier, Cuomo blames unions for only looking out for the teachers and not the students. Furthermore, tenure and pensions are increasingly under attack, in part because eliminating tenure or reducing the pension amounts will reduce the cost of paying teachers, reducing pressure to raise taxes to pay civil servants (Randolph, 2014).

Changing Forms of Governance within Shifting Spatial Scales, Networks Obscure the Ways in Which Markets and Assessment Are Neither Neutral nor Objective

Neoliberals, then, retain dominance because they portray markets and privatization as the natural and neutral way through which decisions should be made. In the remainder of this chapter, I look at the ways in which neoliberals combine the neoliberal social imaginary with changes in governance to gain and retain control.

I first show how education policy is increasingly made at higher spatial scales in society, shifting from the local and provincial/state to the national and international and often outside the traditional political process (Brenner, 2004). Where government was previously characterized by hierarchical decision making, with federal policies trumping state and state trumping local, policy making has become more heterarchical, with decisions made at different levels, often in ways that are less transparent to the public.

Furthermore, notes Brenner (1999), policy making has been transformed through "the accelerated circulation of people, commodities, capital, money, identities and images through global space" and "'supraterritorial' spaces, based upon 'distanceless, borderless interactions' (Scholte, 1996), are decentering the role of territorial and place-based socio-institutional forms" (p. 431). Who and how policy is made has been radically transformed, increasing the power of those who already have the monetary, social, and cultural capital (Bourdieu, 1999). Consequently, formal and informal connections or networks have become more important, and corporations and nonprofit agencies, such as Pearson Inc. and the Bill and Melinda Gates Foundation, have increased their influence on education policy.

Then, I will describe how the older bureaucratic state structures have been replaced by what is described as new public management and their impact on education policy. In particular, new public management aims for efficiency through markets, such as in the creation of charter schools, thereby changing the nature of the relationship between the individual and society. Under neoliberalism, the individual is responsible only for him or herself and, therefore, needs to be entrepreneurial. Furthermore, the emphasis on efficiency and markets promotes quantifying educational activities, leading to, in education, auditing and classifying of students and teachers and collecting and using data as in "data-driven instruction."

Finally, I will highlight some of the ways in which the corporate reforms are contradictory and fail to deliver on their claims. High-stakes testing, the core of the corporate reforms, is promoted as providing objective and useful evaluations of students, teachers, schools, and school districts. However, high-stakes testing, such as New York's Common Core standardized tests, provide very little valid or useful information to students, parents, teachers, or schools. Student, parents, and teachers are not given a specific score for a student, only whether the student has scored at the 3 and 4 levels, which are passing or proficient, or at the 1 and 2 levels, which are failing and not proficient. No information is provided regarding the questions that are on tests and which ones a student answered correctly or incorrectly.

Moreover, whether the test scores rise or fall from one year to the next, either for the state as a whole or schools and school districts, is unknowable given the way in which test results are manipulated. Therefore, the reformers' claims that we need tests to know how well our students are doing are completely misleading. In fact, because so much time is given to preparing for and taking the tests, we know less about our students than if we did not have the tests.

The Demise of Government and the Rise of Governance

Before analyzing these specific changes in governance, I want to make clear what is meant by the shift from government to governance. The notion of government reflects the way in which most people conceptualize how political decisions are made within a democratic society, indeed, the view that is typically taught in textbooks. The traditional view of government focuses on the different scales at which government operates—local, state, and federal—which are responsible for making different kinds of decisions. Further, the relations between organizations at the different scales are hierarchical, with decisions made at the higher levels having precedence over those at lower levels (federal over state and state over local). Government also consists of those who make the policies, often elected—school board members, state and federal representatives, governors, and presidents—and administrators or bureaucrats who implement the policies. Citizens influence policies by voting for school board members, providing testimony and asking questions at school board meetings, and meeting with teachers and school and district administrators.

Over the last several decades, policy making has shifted from the local level to the state, federal, and to what I have described as the national and international levels, in what Brenner (2004) calls the "rescaling of statehood." Some examples of organizations that are both national and international in scope include philanthropic organizations such as the Gates Foundation, which is involved globally in numerous areas, including health and agriculture (Hursh, 2011a); Teach for America, which has similar projects in 36 countries, operating under similar names such as Teach for India or Teach First; corporations, such as Pearson, which as I will describe here and in more depth in chapter 4, that produce most of the textbooks and standardized tests used in the United States; and internationally for the Office for Economic and Cooperative Development (OECD), which is most well known in education circles for creating the Programme for International Student Assessment (PISA) exams.

This rescaling has resulted in policy making becoming less transparent as it is no longer clear where or how policy is made. Most importantly from my viewpoint, the shift from government to governance obscures the process and often disempowers individuals and groups because the number of policy actors has increased and how they influence policy is unclear, and perhaps secret. For example, Bill Gates and the Gates Foundation had a much larger role in developing the Common Core State Standards (CCSS) and curriculum than either the federal or state governments, even though the Gates Foundation had no official responsibility for the CCSS. Consequently, a significant percentage of the public believes that the Common Core is either an initiative of the federal government or a state-lead consortium.

Rizvi and Lingard (2010) reinforce my analysis when they state that national and state governments are no longer the only source of education policies but that the "interests of a whole range of policy actors, both national and international, have become enmeshed in policy processes." Furthermore, "the bureaucratic administrative state also has been replaced by polycentric arrangements involving both public and private interests." And, as I will show, current forms of governance rely on neoliberal notions of society in which government "no longer simply relies on rules and their hierarchical imposition" to regulate individuals but seeks to produce self-regulating, entrepreneurial individuals (p. 117).

The second major change under the shift from government to governance is the decline of the bureaucratic administrative state and the rise of new public management or "corporate managerialism." New public management replaces the older bureaucratic structures that are deemed to be too slow to respond to market pressures. New public management shifts the focus from inputs and processes, including, in education, funding and standards, to outputs and performance to be achieved efficiently through standardized exams and other quantifiable measures. Therefore, new public management provides the rationale for using standardized exams to hold teachers and students accountable. As Rizvi and Lingard (2010) observe, "This has witnessed a new way of steering policy implementation and outcomes through the establishment of objectives and creation of indicators of performance in relation to objectives" (p. 119).

These changes in scale and governance transform both who has the power to make policy and the consequences of policy changes. For example, where the power to make education policy used to reside at the local and provincial/ state levels, and decisions made at the larger scales had precedence over those at the lower (i.e., states over school districts), the shift from hierarchy to heterarchy permits other groups to enter into policy making in ways they did not before. As Ball and Junemann (2012) state:

> [H]eterarchy is an organizational form somewhere between hierarchy and network that draws upon diverse horizontal and vertical links that permit different elements of the policy process to cooperate (and/or compete). Heterarchies have many of the same characteristics of 'assemblages' of and for policy and governance.
>
> (p. 138)

But networks are also increasingly important. Ball and Junemann, in *Networks, New Governance and Education* (2012), undertake an analysis of "the actors and interactions within an across networks, and the 'work' or networking of participating organizations, rather than on network structures, and the distribution of resources" (p. 4). That is, they are more interested in describing how individuals and organizations operate within networks than the networks themselves. Similarly, I am not aiming to conduct an in-depth network analysis of the relationship between the Gates Foundation and the other organizations engaged in corporate reform. Rather, my goal is more limited: to describe, focusing on Bill Gates and the Gates Foundation, how actors bring in different kinds of resources to achieve their ends and that these aims are facilitated by the networks in which people or organizations participate. As described below, the Gates Foundation uses billions of dollars to support people, policies, and organizations to promote and put in place the Common Core standards, curriculum, and assessment.

The Gates Foundation as an Exemplary Case of an Unelected and Unaccountable Nongovernmental Agency Exercising Power Through Heterarchical Networks

Changes in governance have changed the ways in which policy is made, not solely by elected officials but by organizations and individuals who insert themselves within the decision-making process. What this means in practice is that organizations and individuals who previously may not have had access to power now have means to exercise it. We can see this in the impact that Bill Gates had on the development of the Common Core. The Gates Foundation provided an initial $200 million for CCSS when Gene Wilhoit, director of the State School Chiefs, and David Coleman, now head of The College Board, which administers the SAT and Advanced Placement Tests (Lewin, 2012), personally met with Bill Gates and requested his help (Layton, 2014). Gates followed that initial bequest by giving, in June 2009, the National Governors Association $23.6 million to "work with state policy makers on the implementation of the CCSS ... as well as rethinking state policies on teacher effectiveness" (Bill and Melinda Gates Foundation, 2011). From 2009 to the present, Gates gave $147.9 million to the four organizations responsible for CCSS: the National Governors Association, CCSS Organization, Achieve, and Student Achievement Partners. He also gave large sums to the two national teachers' unions, the National Education Association ($4 million) and the American Federation of Teachers ($5.4 million), and to major media organizations such as Education Trust ($2 million), which publishes, among other things, *Education Week*. Gates subsequently funded 1,800 organizations to support the Common Core State Standards (Schneider, 2013).

Gates also uses this funding of organizations to support individuals as key players in creating education policy focusing on standardized testing and school privatization. Administrative personnel move between the Gates Foundation, foundations supported by Gates, and the federal department of education. As just one of many examples that could be given, in 2006 the Gates Foundation gave $30 million to the NewSchools Venture Fund with the goal of developing 200 charter schools (Bill and Melinda Gates Foundation, 2006). The NewSchools Venture Fund "was founded in 1999 with generous backing from venture capitalist John Doerr as well as Cisco CEO John Chambers, Netscape cofounder Jim Clark and others hoping to transform public education Silicon Valley-style" (Periroth, 2011).

Fifteen years later, the fund has invested about $260 million and:

> [R]eceives financing from high-profile education donors like the Broad Foundation, the Bill & Melinda Gates Foundation and the Walton Foundation. On its board are Silicon Valley leaders including John Doerr, partner in the venture capital firm Kleiner Perkins Caulfield & Byers, and Dave

Goldberg, chief executive of Survey Monkey (and husband of Sheryl Sandberg, Facebook's chief operating officer).

(Rich, 2015)

In 2014, the CEO of NewSchools Venture Fund, Ted Mitchell, resigned to become the undersecretary of education under Secretary of Education Arne Duncan. Mitchell's aim is to turn all public schools into charter schools. Mitchell's replacement at NewSchools Venture Fund is Stacey Childress, who was a top official in the Gates Foundation (Cavanagh 2014). Given that my aim is not to do an analysis of the networks in which Gates is a major power broker, only to show that he uses his wealth and connections to advance his agenda, other resources provide a more in-depth analysis of various networks, including Schneider in *A Chronicle of Echoes: Who's Who in the Implosion of American Public Education* (2014). For an excellent "racial-spatial reconstruction" of the "policy ecology of New Orleans public schools," (p. 45) see Buras *Charter Schools, Race, and Urban Space: Where the Market Meets grassroots Resistance* (2015).

As the world's richest person with the world's wealthiest foundation, Gates has access to global leaders in education. Not only does he have direct conduits to the secretary of education but the ear of the United States Senate. In March 2014, he was invited with David Brooks, whose negative view of economic redistribution I described earlier, to address 80 United States Senators over dinner (Brooks, 2014). These changes in the policy process and new methods of governing society reflect shifts from "the government of a unitary state to governance in and by networks" (Bevir & Rhodes, 2003, 41; Ball & Junemann 2012, p. 3).

While policies are developed and implemented in diverse relations and places, they are done so within the neoliberal forms of new public management in which policy actors create policies within "interrelated and mutually reinforcing policy sets" (Ball, Maguire & Braun, 2012, p. 7). It is exactly the interrelated and mutually reinforcing nature of the reform policies that make the corporate reformers so resistant to modifying the standardized testing regimes. Standardized testing makes possible quantified assessments of students, teachers, and schools that then make possible arguments for further privatization. Standardized testing makes it possible to claim that the schools are failing, when more objective assessments such as the NAEP exams suggests that students are, on average, learning more.

The Changing Scales of Governance and Governing Through Standardized Tests: New York, No Child Left Behind, Race to the Top, and Governor Cuomo

In the first chapter, I described the increasing intervention in local education practices such as assessment, curriculum, and pedagogy by those at higher scales, such as the federal government and national and international organizations. In New York, prior to the current corporate reform movement, the State Education

Department was responsible for curriculum and assessment, which included developing the statewide Regents exams, which are subject area final exams. Previous to the recent corporate reform movement, passing these exams was required to earn credit toward a Regents or statewide diploma.

However, as described earlier, in the 1990s these exams became more significant as passing five of them became a requirement to graduate from secondary school. Then, with the passage of NCLB and the subsequent implementation of RTTT, the federal government and other organizations began to have a greater impact on education policy in New York, in particular regarding implementing the Common Core State Standards. Then, most recently with Governor Cuomo's proposals regarding teacher evaluation and tenure, increasing the number of and funding for charter schools, and the funding for private and religious schools, the executive and legislative branches of state government have entered into making education policy that intimately impacts teachers' pedagogical practices (Strauss, 2015a).

In analyzing the rise of both high-stakes testing and the privatization of education both through the creation of curriculum and assessments by other than teachers and the increased funding for and number of charter schools, it becomes clear that the efforts of the neoliberal NGOs, government organizations, foundations, and corporations complement one another. In undertaking such an analysis, Ball invokes the concepts of assemblages and networks. Ball (2012) writes that:

> [P]olicies move through, and are adapted by, networks of social relations or assemblages, involving diverse participants, with a variety of interests, commitments, purposes and influence, which are held together by subscription to a discursive ensemble, which circulates within and is legitimated by these network relations.
>
> (p.11)

Elsewhere, Ball and Junemann (2012) write that the "assemblage articulates, advocates, tests and trials alternative visions of social and education policy . . . based on a diverse but related set of principles" (p. 73). These principles include that society is best served through competitive privatized markets and that students and teachers can be controlled through auditing standardized exams and other quantitative measures. Ball (2008), who has written extensively on the changing nature of governance in education, observes that:

> In policy cycle terms, this is a new type of relationship between the context of policy practice or implementation. This involves steering at a distance via performance measures, (including testing) as a new form of outcomes accountability, as part of the stress on outcomes rather than processes of inputs of the new public management. With this change, more tasks are

devolved to the practice site, but we should not see this as deregulation, but rather as a form of "reregulation."

(Ball, 2008, p. 43)

As I will describe below, under the corporate reforms, teachers' work is increasingly regulated with fewer opportunities to develop and teach their own curriculum. Similarly, the relations between students and their schools are transformed so that students are conceptualized as competitive individuals. Lastly, under market fundamentalism, how individuals conceptualize their relationship is also transformed as people become responsible for their own selves.

Standards and standardized testing enable corporate reformers to regulate teachers from a distance rather than directly because reformers have realized that "what is evaluated is what gets taught." Rather than attempting to directly change curriculum and curriculum standards—an effort that often ends in cultural conflict—they have focused on assessment, in particular standardized tests. In this way, teachers are encouraged but not typically required to teach a standardized curriculum so that their students can do well on the tests. In New York, teachers are not technically required by the State Education Department to specifically teach to the test; indeed, in school districts where the students come from middle-class homes and arrive with significant cultural capital (Barrett & Martina, 2012), teachers may only devote a few weeks to prepping for the standardized exams. But in urban and most school districts, where students may not have the requisite middle-class cultural capital, teachers might devote most or all of the year to specifically preparing students for the testing format and the anticipated content to be assessed.

This tactic has the benefit of limiting teachers without directly controlling them or, as Ball (1994) describes, "governing from a distance" (p. 54). Furthermore, policy makers could often deny responsibility for the tests, even if they had a role in creating and carrying out the policy. For example, New York's commissioner of education, John King (2013), responded to criticisms of the extensive time given to standardized testing by stating it is a federal requirement under Race to the Top and, therefore, out of his control. Further, efforts to adapt the curriculum to a particular school, community, or interest are thwarted by objections that teaching any subject matter that will not be tested undermines the students' chances of doing well on the standardized tests. Consequently, while the curriculum units provided by Engage New York (created by Pearson) were not required, teachers who use Engage New York are less susceptible to criticism than those who use other curricula.

Standardized testing, therefore, significantly transforms education in several key dimensions:

• Standardized testing changes the nature of governance so that teachers are controlled indirectly rather than directly. Standardized tests also promote the notion that teaching and learning can be objectively and numerically assessed and that all that is needed to improve education is to turn schools into competitive markets and students into competitive entrepreneurs.

- Standardized testing transforms the relationship between students, teachers, administrators, and parents into what they can contribute to increasing test scores and narrows teaching to the knowledge and skills likely to be tested.
- Standardized testing transforms the relationship between the individual and society. As Olssen, Codd and O'Neill (2004) describe, neoliberalism changes how individuals conceptualize their relation to society. No longer are they merely making individual choices but they are autonomous entrepreneurs responsible for themselves, their progress and positions, and their own success and failure.

Olssen, Codd and O'Neill (2004) write that:

> Every social transaction is conceptualized as entrepreneurial, to be carried out purely for personal gain. The market introduces competition as the structuring mechanism through which resources and status are allocated efficiently and fairly. The "invisible hand" of the market is thought to be the most efficient way of sorting out what competing individual gets what.
>
> (pp. 137–138)

It becomes the responsibility for students, along with their parents, to choose the best school for themselves; if they fail to thrive, they either need to change schools or work harder. Under market fundamentalism, students have no one to blame for their difficulties but themselves. Furthermore, under neoliberalism, society has no responsibility for the welfare of the individual. Such a view was clearly articulated and stated by former United Kingdom Prime Minister Margaret Thatcher (2011), who in 1987 famously said that, "there was no such thing as society, only individuals" (pp. 626–627). Therefore, individuals are responsible for making choices within free markets; those who are entrepreneurial deserve to succeed, and those who are insufficiently entrepreneurial will fail. Ultimately, each individual is responsible for his or her own fate.

Because for neoliberals everyone is responsible for their own fate, and the government is necessarily inefficient in comparison to markets, neoliberals aim to reduce the role of government and social spending and promote individual responsibility. In the United States, both the Republicans and Democrats have adopted neoliberal policies. Republican politicians have, in general, especially those supported by the Tea Party, aimed to reduce the size of government and governmental spending, except for military expenditures. Some of their goals include eliminating government-funded health care (the Affordable Care Act) and environmental regulations and reducing funding for higher education, medical research, and the transportation infrastructure including roads and bridges (Sachs,

2015). At the same time, Democratic politicians have also supported the neoliberal transformation of education, including Governor Andrew Cuomo; President Obama; and, as CEO of the Chicago Public Schools and as the United States secretary of Education, Arne Duncan.

In this chapter, I have described the ways in which neoliberal governance has transformed how policies are made and who has the power to influence those policies. Furthermore, as I described earlier under the last 40 years of neoliberal policies, economic inequality in the United States has increased and is as great now as any time in the country's history.

Therefore, given the negative transformation of schools and society and the ways in which education and society have become more unequal, we need to examine the discourse and structures that the market fundamentalists have used to advance the reregulation and privatization of schools.

Neoliberal Reforms: Failed Promises, Manipulated Outcomes

Corporate reformers have justified their reform proposals as fulfilling students' civil right to a quality education and that charter schools will provide students with a better education, therefore serving as the "great equalizer." Corporate reformers frequently claim that "poverty is not an excuse for students failing to learn," and, therefore, providing a better education will reduce poverty and inequality. Lastly, they argue that standardized testing is also a civil right that provides students and families with objective information about the students, their teachers, and schools. However, as I will show, none of these claims are true.

From the beginning, high-stakes testing has been promoted as giving students and parents objective data that teachers were not providing. In *No Child Left Behind: A Parents Guide* (U.S. Department of Education, 2003), parents are told that standardized tests are a valid and reliable means of assessing students' learning, superior to teacher-generated assessments. *The Guide* advises parents that NCLB "will give them objective data" through standardized testing (p. 12). Further, objective data from tests is necessary because "many parents have children who are getting straight As, but find out too late that their child is not prepared for college. That's just one reason why NCLB gives parents objective data about how their children are doing" (p. 12). Teachers, NCLB strongly implies, have not rigorously enforced standards nor accurately assessed students, therefore covering up their own and their students' failures. Further, test scores are useful to parents because "parents will know how well learning is occurring in their child's class. They will know information on how their child is progressing compared to other children" (p. 9). Because teachers, NCLB claims, have relied too often on their own assessments, standardized test scores will also benefit them. NCLB "provides teachers with independent information about each child's strengths and weaknesses. With this knowledge, teachers can craft lessons to make sure each student meets or exceeds standards" (p. 9).

In the current debate in New York over parents opting their children out of the Common Core standardized tests, Chancellor Tisch argues that opting children out of the test will eliminate having an "objective measure" of student learning, which will "make it easy to ignore the achievement gap between students of color and white students." Furthermore, the tests make it possible for parents to "know whether his or her child is on track for success in the fifth grade or high school graduation or success in college." Like Cuomo, she claims, "It's time to stop making noise to protect the adults and start speaking up for the students" (Tisch, 2015). She ignores, as I will show, that the test scores provide only whether students are scoring a 1, 2, 3, or 4 on the tests and that the scores are manipulated so that, whether the scores rise or fall, they tell us nothing.

Similarly, Bush's secretary of education, Rodney Paige (Paige & Jackson, 2004), Michael Bloomberg, the previous mayor of New York City, and New York's current governor, Andrew Cuomo, have all extended the argument beyond providing objective assessments to positively compare their agenda of high-stakes testing and privatization to the Civil Rights Movement of the 1960s.

However, in New York, as soon as standardized testing became high stakes, commissioners of education began manipulating the test results. Sometimes, the test scores are manipulated to produce a high failure rate so that the public schools can be portrayed as failing, as in the case of the most recent Common Core exam results, or to portray the commissioner and regents as having high standards. But, as the past president of the American Education Research Association, Linn (2003), revealed over a decade ago, at some point commissioners and other officials want to demonstrate that their reforms are working and therefore increase the passing rate by making the scoring easier. Let me give some examples.

As I described in chapter 1, the first instantiation of high-stakes testing in New York was the requirement, beginning in the mid-1990s, that students pass five Regents exams in four different subjects: science, social studies, math, and English. In English, math, and science, the students need only pass one of the several subject area exams and, therefore, are most likely to take the exam offered in the lowest grade, which in science is the biology of "living environments" exam. Given that the commissioners' desire to both appear to be raising standards and at the same time more students have graduate, the State Education Department made it easier for students to pass by lowering the cut score. For example, a decade ago the biology or "living environments" exam was criticized as being too easy, as students needed to answer only 39% of the questions correctly to earn a passing grade of 55% (Cala, 2003). The practice has not substantially changed over the last decade. My analysis two years ago of the scoring rubrics on the NYSED website revealed that to pass, students needed correct answers on only 47% of the multiple-choice questions on the living environments exam and 53% correct on the algebra exam.

Conversely, the exams for the advanced, nonrequired courses, such as physics and chemistry, have sometimes been made more difficult. In 2003, 39% of students failed the physics exam, in order, critics charged, to make regents testing appear more rigorous (Winerip, 2003). Commissioner Mills apparently assumed that since students did not need to pass the physics exam to graduate, a high failure rate would be of little concern to the students and their families. However, he seems to have been unaware that because most of the students who enroll in physics are academically successful middle- and upper-class students applying for university, and low or failing grades on the state physics exam harms their chances for admission, the students and their parents responded by pressuring the State Education Department to change the scoring. At first, Commissioner Mills defended the results as "statistically sound" (Dillon, 2003; Winerip, 2011, p. 27), but the test results were so dubious the State Council of Superintendents sent letters to universities urging them to disregard the test results (Ravitch, 2015a). Finally, revelations on how the scores were manipulated to yield a low passing rate left the commissioner with no choice but to respond to public pressure by resetting the cut score and thereby substantially raising the scores (Winerip, 2003).

High-stakes standardized testing extended beyond the high school regents courses when No Child Left Behind began requiring tests in grades three through eight in 2002. While the results on the secondary schools exams have fluctuated, the scores on the elementary grade exams have generally, until recently, steadily risen at rates of questionable validity. In the same way that scores on the regents exams have been manipulated by raising or lowering the cut scores, the minimum scores necessary to reach increased levels of proficiency on the math and reading tests required under NCLB have consistently declined, therefore resulting in students' passing rates increasing. Ravitch, in *The Death and Life of the Great American School System: How Testing and Choice Are Undermining Education* (2010), points out how much easier it has become for New York's elementary students to score in the top three of four levels on the standardized tests. She wrote:

> On the sixth-grade reading test in 2006, students needed to earn 36.2% of the points to attain level 2; by 2009, students in that grade need only 17.9%. In seventh grade math, students needed to earn 36.2% of the points on the test to advance to level 2 in 2006, but by 2009, they needed to earn only 22%. The standards to advance from level 1 to level 2 dropped so low that many students could get enough correct answers to pass to level 2 by randomly guessing.
>
> (Ravitch, 2010, p. 79)

Winerip (2011) undertook research similar to Ravitch's and reported that in 2005, "New York City fourth graders made record gains on the state English test, with 59% scoring proficient, compared with 49% the year before." Similarly, in

"2008 math scores for grades three through eight indicate that 89.7% are proficient, up from 72.% in 2007" (Winerip, 2011, p. 27).

That these improvements in student learning are deceptive is also revealed when the results on New York State's tests are compared with New York State's students' scores on the more statistically sound NAEP English and math exams. The NAEP exams are administered every other year to statistically representative samples of students in fourth, eighth, and twelfth grades, and the results can be compared from year to year. In 2005, only 19% of the New York City students were proficient on the eighth-grade reading test, compared to 22% two years before; by 2009, the test results were the lowest in a decade. By November 2011, "New York [was] one of two states in the nation to post statistically significantly declines on the National Assessment [NAEP] tests" (Winerip, 2011, p. 19). While the percentage of students passing the New York State exams was rising, a lower percentage of students were passing the NAEP exams, providing evidence that the improvements may be more of a mirage than real.

Whenever questions are raised regarding the validity of the state tests, the commissioners and chancellors defend them as rigorous and statistically sound. In New York City, Mayor Bloomberg used the improving test results to successfully lobby the state legislature to renew mayoral control of the schools and to win reelection. Finally, in June 2010, Merryl Tisch, the chancellor of the Board of Regents, who continually defends the tests as objective in spite of her admissions that they are not, admitted that the state test scores were ridiculously inflated and should not be believed, and test scores were rescaled so that approximately one-third fewer students scored at the proficiency level. For example, the 68.8% English proficiency rates was immediately rescaled to 42.4% (Winerip, 2011). Of course, Tisch's amnesia regarding the validity of the test scores serves a purpose. By rescaling the scores so that fewer students are proficient, the commissioner can then start rescaling them again to show improvement, for which the commissioner and the chancellor can and do take credit (Linn, 2003).

The manipulation of test scores continues with the Common Core State Standards tests. As Burris, an award-winning high school principal in New York observes, the cut scores were set to yield a 31% passing rate (Strauss, 2015b). Given that after the test was administered the students' passing rate matched the percentage desired by the commissioner, Burris observed that, "the kids did not even need to show up for the test" (2014). Urban districts had very low passing rates. The Rochester City School District (RCSD) had a 5% pass rate, which was the lowest in the state.

As with past test results, those in power use the test scores to advance their own cause and careers. For example, Michael Bloomberg, who during his last mayoral campaign took credit for improving test results, described the low percentage of city children classified as proficient as "some very good news" (Pallas, 2013), and Commissioner King called the results "a good thing" (New and Notes, 2013). Amazingly, both Chancellor Tisch and Commissioner King promised that the percentage of students scoring as proficient would be higher, in part no doubt because they can just lower the cut score to yield a higher passing rate. However, they would not increase the passing rate too much because then the Common Core results will not be believable in the same way the math and language arts results became "unbelievable." One might predict the scores would improve but not by much. And, in fact, when the second year test scores were released in summer 2014, that is exactly what happened (Weiner, 2014).

So the scores are manipulated for political purposes, and politicians like Bloomberg can spin rising or falling test scores as "good news." What is the purpose of the tests? What does high-stakes testing do? In this section, I want to argue that standardized tests are intentionally used and misused to blame public (primarily urban) schools and school teachers for the shortcomings of education so that corporate reformers can push privatizing schools (by either converting them to charter schools or turning over their management and operation to for-profit companies) and shift the blame for increasing inequality onto the schools rather than where it should belong: neoliberal economic and social policies (Apple, 1996a).

We can see how this plays out in the Rochester City School District (RCSD). As noted above, only 5% of RCSD students were proficient on the recent Common Core assessments, which have ramifications for the teachers, students, schools, and school districts. First, in order to receive RTTT funding, the state agreed that teachers will be evaluated as failing ("ineffective" or "developing") or passing ("effective" or "very effective") based largely on their students' test scores as part of their Annual Professional Performance Review (APPR). Teachers who are determined to be failing are required to develop a Teaching Improvement Plan (Strauss, 2011).

In an urban district like Rochester, the students' low test scores resulted in 922 of the 2,474 RCSD teachers (or 37%) receiving ratings of "developing" or "ineffective," all of whom now require a professional development plan. According to the union's agreement with the State Education Department, if the teachers are rated as failing for two consecutive years, proceedings to terminate their employment can begin. However, as I describe later, under the recent reforms initiated under Cuomo, any teacher in any district who is rated as "failing" for two consecutive years can have proceedings begun to remove them from their position. They also are no longer eligible to begin tenure proceedings for five years, a clock that would be restarted if at any time in six years they received another low rating. Adam Urbanski, president of the Rochester Teachers Association, stated, "APPR was intentionally positioned to dismantle urban public schools—possibly to diminish union power—and allow for the growth of charter schools" (Macaluso, 2013b).

Urbanski's observation is backed up by two events regarding the school district's future. Soon after the test scores were made public, Governor Cuomo declared that low-scoring school districts might suffer the "death penalty." Subsequently, the then commissioner of education, John King, began "pushing for a bill that would allow the Board of Regents to take over school districts with histories of low academic performance or financial problems" (Macaluso, 2013a). That legislation was introduced as part of the state's annual budget on the day before the budget was due, passed, and signed into law (Ravitch 2015b). Fifteen Rochester public schools are now threatened with takeover "by a third party [who] would have broad authority, with the ability to do everything from extending the academic day to converting the struggling school into a publicly funded, privately funded charter school" (Campbell, 2015). In fact, the legislation states that whoever the school is handed over to, and it could be a single individual, has the right to cancel all contracts, including with the unions, and hire and fire whomever they want, without oversight from the school district. They will have absolute authority over a publicly funded school. Said Cuomo, "when it comes to education, the budget we approved will transform our school system in comprehensive ways. The reforms we have included will move us to an education system that rewards results, addresses challenges and demands accountability" (Campbell, 2015).

The low percentage of urban students scoring as proficient on the tests also provides a rationale for charter school operators to increase their number. Joe Klein, who owns Klein Steel in Rochester and was a former board member of True North Rochester Preparatory Program, a charter school, has created a nonprofit company to recruit charter schools to Rochester. He has used the low-test scores to legitimize charter schools and developed a partnership with the Rochester Institute of Technology to operate charter schools. He recently stated, "In Rochester you get 5% proficiency rates. Obviously, it's not working. You can go to Rochester Prep and see those same kids thriving. I think you will start to see every university involved with a high-quality charter school" (Lankes, 2013, p. 5A).

The above discussion regarding the political manipulation of test scores and their use and misuse demonstrates how test scores can organize how we think about the world. Ball (2013) writes, "Discourse is related directly to power, to regimes of truth and grids of specification—the dividing, classifying, and relating together objects of discourse" (pp. 23–24). As we can see, the test scores serve to describe students as more or less successful, without any connection to what students were also learning. Furthermore, at least in part because most people are unaware of the way that test scores have been manipulated at the whim of the commissioner or chancellor, they assume that the numbers tell us something about student learning, when they really say something about the commissioner and chancellor.

As Ball (2013) further describes:

> Here we see again the relations between the delimitation and constitution of a field of knowledge in relation to a form of expertise—statistics—that . . . creates and legitimates new sites of truth. This "making up of people" consists

of what Hacking (1995) identifies as five interactive elements—classification, people (the subject of measurement), institutions, knowledge, and expert.

(p. 74)

Ball continues by describing how testing aims to "represent reality in terms of quantifiable and manipulable domains, and thus render reality as a field of government" (p. 74); that is, policies and practices are developed to improve test scores rather than to positively affect what occurs in classrooms and schools. Rather than discussing what is worth learning; whether teachers are developing curriculum and pedagogical practices that promote learning; how we can assess that learning; and its value to the community that consists of school, neighborhood, nation, and world, the conversation focuses on the so-called failure of teachers, students, and schools and how privatizing test development and scoring, school management, and whole schools as charters can remedy the problem.

Not only does high-stakes testing limit the ways in which we conceptualize schooling, it also limits how we conceptualize education within society as a whole. Again, Ball (2013) writes:

> This "grid of social regularities" constitutes "what becomes socially visible as a social problem and what becomes socially visible as a range of credible solutions" (Sheurich, 1994, p. 301)—the possible and the impossible (what actors do not think about)—and thus the objects, subjects, and concepts that policies form and regulate.
>
> (p. 23)

The focus on test scores promotes discourses that objectify students and teachers as failing and limit our ability to imagine what could be done to improve student learning. Such discourses also undermine our ability to focus on the factors that most affect educational outcomes: poverty and lack of jobs and social services, factors that have been exacerbated under neoliberalism.

In the next chapter, I describe the ways in which supporters of the corporate reform agenda in New York broadened the use of standardized test scores and the discourse of neoliberalism to undercut public education and the teaching profession.

References

Apple, M. (1996a). *Cultural Politics and Education*. New York: Teachers College Press.

Apple, M. (1996b, June 30). Being popular about national standards: A review of *National Standards in American Education: A Citizen's Guide. Education Policy Analysis Archives* 4(10), 1–6. Retrieved from http://usf.sobek.ufl.edu/content/SF/S0/02/45/11/00059/E11-00059.pdf

Ball, S.J. (1994). *Education Reform: A Critical and Post-Structural Approach*. Buckingham, England: Open University Press.

Ball, S. J. (2008). *The Education Debate*. Bristol, UK: Policy Press.

Ball, S. J. (2012). *Global Education, Inc.: New Policy Networks and the Neoliberal Imaginary*. New York: Routledge.

Ball, S.J. (2013). *Foucault, Power, and Education*. New York: Routledge.

Ball, S. J. (2015). Education, governance and the tyranny of numbers. *Journal of Education Policy, 30*(3), 299–301. Retrieved from http://dx.doi.org/10.1080/02680939.2015.1013271

Ball, S. J. & Junemann, C. (2012). *Networks, New Governance and Education*. Bristol, UK: Policy Press.

Ball, S. J., Maguire, M., & Braun, A. (2012). *How Schools Do Policy: Policy Enactments in Secondary Schools*. New York: Routledge.

Barken, J. (2013, Fall). Plutocrats at work: How big philanthropy undermines democracy. *Dissent*. Retrieved from http://www.dissentmagazine.org/article/plutocrats-at-work-how-big-philanthropy-undermines-democracy

Barrett, B. D. & Martina, C. M. (2012). Towards a non-deterministic reading of Pierre Bourdieu: habitus and educational change in urban schools. *Policy Futures in Education, 10*(3), 249–262.

Berliner, D. C. (2013). Effects of inequality and poverty vs. teachers and schooling on America's youth. *Teachers College Record, 115*(12). Retrieved from http://www.tcrecord.org (ID no. 16889)

Berliner, D. C. (2014). *50 Myths and Lies that Threaten America's Public Schools: The Real Crisis in Education*. New York: Teachers College Press.

Berliner, D. C. & Biddle, B. (1995). *The Manufactured Crisis: Myths, Fraud, and the Attack on America's Public Schools*. Reading, MA: Addison Wesley.

Bevir, M. & Rhodes, R. A. W. (2003). Searching for civil society: Changing patterns of governance in Britain. *Public Administration, 81*(1), 41–62.

Bill and Melinda Gates Foundation (2006, October 9). Major new investment supports NewSchools Venture Fund's efforts to provide 200 high-quality charter schools for 100,000 low-income students. Bill and Melinda Gates Foundation website. Retrieved from http://www.gatesfoundation.org/Media-Center/Press-Releases/2006/10/Major-New-Investment-Supports-NewSchools-Venture-Funds-Efforts-to-Provide-200-HighQuality-Charter-Schools-for-100000-LowIncome-Students

Bill and Melinda Gates Foundation. (2011, February). National Governors Association Center for Best Practices. Retrieved from www.gatesfoundations.org/How-We-Work/QuickLinks/Grants-Database/Grants/2011/02/OPP1031924.

Blain, G. & Lovett, K. (2015, January 21). Andrew Cuomo unveils big education plan, budget proposal in annual "state of the state" address. *Daily News*. Retrieved from http://www.nydailynews.com/news/politics/cuomo-unveils-big-education-plan-state-state-talk-article-1.2086990

Block, F. & Somers, M. (2014). *The Power of Market Fundamentalism*. Cambridge, MA: Harvard University Press.

Bourdieu, P. (1999). *Acts of Resistance: Against the Tyranny of the State*. New York: The New Press.

Brenner, N. (1999). Globalization as reterritorialisation: The re-scaling of urban governance in the European Union. *Urban Studies, 36*(3), 431–451.

Brenner, N. (2004). *New State Spaces: Urban Governance and the Rescaling of Statehood*. Oxford: Oxford University Press.

Brooks, D. (2014, April 17). When the circus descends. *The New York Times*, A23. Retrieved from http://www.nytimes.com/2014/04/18/opinion/brooks-when-the-circus-descends.html

Brooks. D. (2015, March 6). The temptation of Hilary. *The New York Times,* A26.

Buras, K.L. (2014, December 26). Charter schools flood New Orleans. *The Progressive*. Retrieved from http://www.progressive.org/news/2014/12/187949/charter-schools-flood-new-orleans

Buras, K.L. (2015). *Charter Schools, Race, and Urban Space: Where the Market Meets Grassroots Resistance*. New York: Routledge.

Cala, W. (2003, October 22). Testimony before the New York Senate Standing Committee on Education, Roosevelt Hearing Room C, Legislative Office Building, Albany, New York. Retrieved June 10, 2014, from http://www.timeoutfromtesting.org/testi monies/1022_Testimony_Cala.pdf

Campbell, J. (2015, April 6). Some Rochester schools could face takeover. *Democrat and Chronicle*. Retrieved from http://www.democratandchronicle.com/story/news/2015/ 04/06/school-takeover-new-york-state/25382697/

Cavanagh, S. (2014, May 13). A top Gates Foundation official leaving for New Schools Venture Fund. *Education Week*. Retrieved from http://blogs.edweek.org/edweek/mar ketplacek12/2014/05/top_gates_foundation_official_leaves_for_newschools_ven ture_fund.html

Cuomo, A.W. (2014, March 4). Video and transcript. Gov. Cuomo at charter school rally: Education is about the students, and the students come first. Governor Cuomo website. Retrieved from https://www.governor.ny.gov/news/video-transcript-gov-cuomo- charter-school-rally-education-about-students-and-students-com

Delevingne, L. (2015, March 11). Companies cash in on Common Core despite controversy. *CNBC*. Retrieved from http://www.cnbc.com/id/102496406

Dewey, J. (1915). *The Child and the Curriculum and the School and Society*. Chicago: University of Chicago Press.

Dewey, J. (1963). *Education and Experience*. New York: Macmillan/Collier (originally published in 1938).

Dillon, S. (2003, July 18). Outcry over Regents physics test. But officials in Albany won't budge. *The New York Times*. Retrieved June 10, 2014, from http://www.nytimes. com/2003/07/18/nyregion/outcry-over-regents-physics-test-but-officials-in-albany- won-t-budge.html?pagewanted=all&src=pm

Ebenstein, L. (2007). *Milton Friedman: A Biography*. New York: Palgrave Macmillan.

Fones-Wolf, E. (1994). *Selling Free Enterprise: The Business Assault on Labor and Liberalism 1945–1960*. Urbana: University of Illinois Press.

Friedman, M. (1952). *Essays on Positive Economics*. Chicago: University of Chicago Press.

Friedman, M. (1962). *Capitalism and Freedom*. Chicago: University of Chicago Press.

Friedman, T.L. (1999). *The Lexus and the Olive Tree*. New York: Farrar, Straus, and Giroux.

Friedman, T. L. (1999). *The World is Flat: A Brief History of the Twenty-first Century*. New York: Farrar, Straus, and Giroux.

Fukuyama, F. (1992). *The End of History and the Last Man*. New York: The Free Press.

Gilson, D. (2011, July, August). Overworked America: 12 charts that will make your blood boil. *Mother Jones*. Retrieved from http://www.motherjones.com/politics/2011/06/ speedup-americans-working-harder-charts

Harvey, D. (2005). *A Brief History of Neoliberalism*. Oxford: Oxford University Press.

Hayek, F.A. (1944). *The Road to Serfdom*. Chicago: University of Chicago Press.

Hayek, F.A. (1960). *The Constitution of Liberty*. Chicago: University of Chicago Press.

Henderson, J.A. & Hursh, D. (2014). Economics and education for human flourishing: Wendell Berry and the *Oikonomic* Alternative to Neoliberalism. *Educational Studies*, 167–186.

Hursh, D. (2008). *High-Stakes Testing and the Decline of Teaching and Learning*. Lanham, MD: Rowman & Littlefield.

Hursh, D. (2011a). The Gates Foundation's interventions into education, health, and food policies: Technology, power, and the privatization of public problems. In P.E. Kovacs (ed.), *The Gates Foundation and the Future of U.S. "Public" Schools*, 39–52. New York: Routledge.

Hursh, D. (2011b). More of the same: How free market capitalism dominates the economy and education. In P. Carr & B. Porfilio (eds.), *The Phenomenon of Obama and the Agenda for Education: Can Hope Audaciously Trump Neoliberalism?* Charlotte, NC: Information Age Press, 3–22.

Judt, T. (2010). *Ill Fares the Land.* New York: Penguin Books.

Kaplan, T. & Taylor, K. (2012, January 17). Invoking King, Cuomo and Bloomberg stoke fight on teacher review impasse. *The New York Times*, A17.

King, J. (2013, November 7). Forum on the Common Core. Brighton High School, Brighton, New York.

Kovacs, P.E. (Ed.). 2011. *The Gates Foundation and the Future of U.S. "Public" Schools.* New York: Routledge.

Kruse, K. M. (2015). *One Nation under God: How Corporate America Invented Christian America.* New York: Perseus Books Group.

Lankes, S. (2013, September 9). Charter school, RIT join effort: College to work with new city high school. *Democrat and Chronicle*, 1A, 5A.

Layton, L. (2014, June 7). How Bill Gates pulled off the swift Common Core revolution. *The Washington Post.* Retrieved from http://www.washingtonpost.com/politics/how-bill-gates-pulled-off-the-swift-common-core-revolution/2014/06/07/a830e32e-ec34-11e3-9f5c-9075d5508f0a_story.html

Lewin, T. (2012, May 16). Backer of the Common Core School curriculum is chosen to head the College Board. *The New York Times.* Retrieved from http://www.nytimes.com/2012/05/16/education/david-coleman-to-lead-college-board.html

Linn, R. (2003). Accountability: Responsibility and reasonable expectations. *Educational Researcher, 32*(7), 3–13.

Lipman, P. (2007). From accountability to privatization and African-American exclusion: Chicago's "Renaissance 2010." *Educational Policy 21*(3), 471–502. doi:10.1177/08959 04806297734

Macaluso, T.L. (2013a, August 16). Albany is going to fix urban schools. *City Newspaper.* Retrieved June 10, 2014, from http://www.rochestercitynewspaper.com/NewsBlog/archives/2013/08/16/albany-is-going-to-fix-urban-schools

Macaluso, T.L. (2013b, October 2). Hundreds of teachers appealing APPR. *City Newspaper.* Retrieved June 10, 2014, from http://www.rochestercitynewspaper.com/NewsBlog/archives/2013/10/02/hundreds-of-city-teachers-appealing-appr

Marsh, D. & Smith, M. (2000). Understanding policy networks: Towards a dialectical approach. *Political Studies, 48*, 4–21.

McKinley, J. (2015, March 10). Assembly Democrats reject Cuomo's education reform plans. New York Times. A17. http://www.nytimes.com/2015/03/10/nyregion/assembly-democrats-reject-cuomos-education-reform-plans.html

Milne, S. (2014, October 3). During the miners' strike, Thatcher's secret state was the real enemy within. *The Guardian.* Retrieved from http://www.theguardian.com/commentis free/2014/oct/03/miners-strike-thatcher-real-enemy-within-extremism

National Academy of Sciences, National Academy of Engineering, and Institute of Medicine. (2007). *Rising Above the Gathering Storm: Energizing and Employing America for a Brighter Future Written by the Committee on Prospering in the Global Economy of the 21st Century.* Washington, DC: The National Academies Press. Retrieved from http://www.nap.edu/catalog/11463/rising-above-the-gathering-storm-energizing-and-employing-america-for

National Center for Education Statistics. (2015). The history of NAEP contractors: Current NAPE contractors. Pearson. Retrieved from http://nces.ed.gov/nationsreportcard/contracts/history.aspx

National Commission on Excellence in Education. (1983). *A Nation at Risk: A Report to the Nation and the Secretary of Education.* Washington, DC: U.S. Department of Education.

News and Notes from Commissioner King. (2013, August 19). *NYSED* website. Retrieved from http://myemail.constantcontact.com/News-and-Notes-from-Commissioner-King.html?soid=1110847617454&aid=2jRkW5otDjg

Odato, J.M. (2013, November 25). Education reform backed by the wealthy. *Times Union.* Retrieved from http://www.timesunion.com/local/article/Wealth-backs-reform-team-5006670.php

Olssen, M., Codd, J. & O'Neill., A. M. (2004). *Education Policy: Globalization, Citizenship, and Democracy.* Thousand Oaks, CA: Sage.

Paige, R. & Jackson, A. (2004, November 8). Education: The civil-rights issue of the twenty-first century. *Hispanic Vista.* Retrieved from http://hispanicvista.com/HVC/Opinion/Guest-Columns/1108Rod_Paige-Alponso_Jackson.htm

Pallas, A. (2013, August 8). The envelope please. *A sociological eye on education.* Retrieved June 10, 2014, from http://eyeoned.org/content/the-envelope-please_501/

Peck, J. (2010). *Constructions of Neoliberalism.* Oxford: Oxford University Press.

Periroth, N. (2011, September, 19). New Schools CEO Ted Mitchell: My best idea for k-12 education. *Forbes.* Retrieved from http://www.forbes.com/sites/nicoleperlroth/2011/09/19/newschools-ceo-ted-mitchell-my-best-idea-for-k-12-education/

Powell, L. (1971, August 23). The Powell Memo. Retrieved from http://reclaimdemocracy.org/powell_memo_lewis/

Randolph, E. (2014, June 2). Is Andrew Cuomo liberal? *The New York Times.* Retrieved from http://takingnote.blogs.nytimes.com/2014/06/02/is-andrew-cuomo-liberal/

Ranelagh, J. (1992). *Thatcher's People.* London: Fontana.

Ravitch, D. (2010). *The Death and Life of the Great American School System: How Testing and Choice Are Undermining Education.* New York: Basic Books.

Ravitch, D. (2014a, September 10). The crisis in our schools: Is there a future for public education? Skype presentation at East High School, Rochester, New York.

Ravitch, D. (2014b, December 2). Pearson created the International PISA test for 2015. Retrieved from http://dianeravitch.net/2014/12/02/pearson-created-the-international-pisa-test-for-2015/

Ravitch, D. (2014c, December 30). Beware the language of "reform" that isn't about reform. Diane Ravitch's blog. Retrieved from http://dianeravitch.net/2014/12/30/beware-the-language-of-reform-that-isnt-about-reform/

Ravitch, D. (2015a, March 29). Nearly 100 Superintendents Sign Petition to Save Public Education in NY. Retrieved from http://dianeravitch.net/2015/03/29/nearly-100-su perintendents-sign-petition-to-save-public-education-in-ny/

Ravitch, D. (2015b, April 11). New York Senate wall of shame and wall of fame. Retrieved from http://dianeravitch.net/2015/04/11/new-york-senate-wall-of-shame-and-wall-of-fame/

Rich, M. (2015, January 16). Percentage of poor student in public schools rises. *The New York Times.* Retrieved from http://www.nytimes.com/2015/01/17/us/school-poverty-study-southern-education-foundation.html

Rizvi, F. & Lingard, B. (2010). *Globalizing Education Policy.* New York: Routledge.

Sachs, J. (2015, March 10). By separating nature from economics, we have walked blindly into tragedy. *The Guardian.* Retrieved from http://www.theguardian.com/global-development-professionals-network/2015/mar/10/jeffrey-sachs-economic-policy-climate-change

Saltman, K.J. (Ed.). (2007). *Schooling and the Politics of Disaster.* New York: Routledge.

Saltman, K.J. (2010). *The Gift of Education: Public Education and Venture Philanthropy.* New York: Palgrave.

Saltman, K.J. (2012). *The Failure of Corporate School Reform.* Boulder, CO: Paradigm.

Scheurich, J.J. (1994). Policy archaeology: A new policy studies methodology. *Journal of Education Policy, 9*(4), 297–316.

Schneider, M. K. (2013, August 27). A brief audit of Bill Gate's Common Core spending. Retrieved from https://deutsch29.wordpress.com/2013/08/27/a-brief-audit-of-bill-gates-common-core-spending/

Schneider, M. K. (2014). *A Chronicle of Echoes: Who's who in the Implosion of American Public Education.* Charlotte, NC: Information Age Publishing.

Scholte, J.A. (1996). The geography of collective identities in a globalizing world. *Review of International Political Economy 3*(4), 565–607.

Simon, S. (2015, February 10). No profit left behind. *Politico.* Retrieved from http://www.politico.com/story/2015/02/pearson-education-115026.html

Snedden, D. (1915). Vocational education. *New Republic, 3,* 40–2.

Snedden, D. (1924, November 1). Education for a world of team-players and team workers. *School and Society, 20,* 554–56.

Strauss, V. (2011, December 7). Are half of New York's teachers really "not effective"? *The Washington Post.* Retrieved December 7, 2011, from http://www.washingtonpost.com/blogs/answer-sheet/post/are-half-of-new-yorks-teachers-really-not-effective/2011/12/05/gIQAhDXyaO_blog.html

Strauss, V. (2015a, January 1). Teacher evaluation: Going from bad to worse? *The Washington Post.* Retrieved from http://www.washingtonpost.com/blogs/answer-sheet/wp/2015/01/01/teacher-evaluation-going-from-bad-to-worse/

Strauss, V. (2015b, April 29). The scary way Common Core test "cut scores" are selected. *The Washington Post.* Retrieved from http://www.washingtonpost.com/blogs/answer-sheet/wp/2014/04/29/the-scary-way-common-core-test-cut-scores-are-selected/

Taylor, C. (2004). *Modern Social Imaginaries.* Durham, NC: Duke University Press.

Teachout, Z. & Khan, M. (2014, December 2). Corruption in New York: Hedge funds and the takeover of New York's schools. *The Washington Park Project.* Retrieved from http://www.aqeny.org/wp-content/uploads/2014/12/Hedge-Fund-White-Paper-Teachout-Final-Formatted-2.pdf

Thatcher. M. (2011). *The Downing Street Years.* New York: Harper Collins. Retrieved from http://www.margaretthatcher.org/speeches/displaydocument.asp?docid=106689

Tisch, M. H. (2015, April 7). Will the opt-out movement hurt kids who need help the most? *The Hechingerreport.* Retrieved from http://hechingerreport.org/will-the-opt-out-movement-hurt-kids-who-need-help-the-most/

US Department of Education, Office of the Secretary. (2003). *NCLB: A parents guide to NCLB: What to know and where to go.* Washington, DC: Author.

Vilas. C. (1996). Neoliberal social policy: Managing poverty (somehow). *NACLA Report on the Americas, 29*(20), 16–21.

Weiner, R. (2014, August 15). Common Core test barely rise in 2nd year. *Lohud: The Journal News.* http://www.lohud.com/story/news/education/2014/08/14/common-core-tests-ela-flat-math-scores-nd-year/14074893/

Winerip, M. (2003, March 12). Passing grade defies laws of physics. *The New York Times,* A22, B7. Retrieved from http://www.nytimes.com/2003/03/12/nyregion/on-education-when-a-passing-grade-defies-laws-of-physics.html?src=pm

Winerip, M. (2011, December 19). 10 years of assessing students with scientific exactitude. *The New York Times,* A24.

Yerkes, R. (1919, February 15). The mental rating of school children. *National School Service, 1*(12), 6–7.

3

GOVERNOR CUOMO AND THE NEOLIBERAL ATTACK ON PUBLIC SCHOOLS, TEACHERS, AND UNIONS

In the previous chapters, I described how, in New York, the tests have become increasingly high stakes, first under new requirements from the Board of Regents, then under NCLB, and most recently under RTTT. In this chapter, I will present evidence for how, over the last 15 years, corporate reforms have encompassed a widening range of reforms, including evaluating teachers through standardized test scores, privatizing the developing of curriculum and assessments, and promoting charter schools. I will begin by describing the primary effects of the federal law known as NCLB; the Obama initiative known as RTTT, which provides funding to states through "competitive grants" (U.S. Department of Education, n.d.); and, finally, Governor Cuomo's recent education reform proposals.

After presenting these reforms, I will show how the reforms are part of a larger effort to turn education into a profit-making industry and are promoted by those who desire to profit financially from the changes. I argue that understanding the motives behind these proposals that aim to restrict teacher autonomy and open up opportunities to invest in and profit from privatization requires understanding the financialization of education: the ways in which the government has made education an area of investment and the ways in which Wall Street and the wealthy aim to benefit from its privatization. Therefore, I detail how Cuomo's connections to charter school CEOs and billionaire hedge fund managers impact Cuomo's agenda regarding the privatization of public schools.

Subsequently, when Cuomo tells us that he aims to destroy the "public school monopoly" because he is the only one that cares about the students, I argue that the opposite is the case. His reforms are motivated not by caring about the students but by a desire to provide investment opportunities and tax breaks to the lobby groups and hedge fund managers who have contributed to his and his allies' political campaigns.

Cuomo also aims to mislead the public when he claims that the public schools are failing because the teachers only care about their own careers and their pensions. He says that teachers are resisting evaluation—"they don't want to be evaluated, I understand that"—and are formenting parental resistance to the Common Core State Standards (CCSS) and standardized tests (Lovett, 2014).

However, on the whole, it is not the teachers that are failing; under the current regime of high-stakes testing, they struggle to retain some professional autonomy. Rather, Cuomo has significantly underfunded the public schools by not complying with the lawsuit won by the Campaign for Equity in 2006 that required the state to increase funding so as to provide a "sound basic education" (Education Law Center, 2015).

Furthermore, in 2009, Cuomo used the economic recession to impose an austerity budget on the public schools. He significantly reduced state funding for the public schools under the oddly named Gap Elimination Adjustment. According to a recent study, the school districts in Monroe County, where Rochester is located, received more than $443 million less in state aid than they should have over the last five years (McDermott, 2015). These funding cuts occurred even though the previous governor, Eliot Spitzer, and the legislature created:

> [O]ne statewide school aid formula based on student poverty concentration and district wealth and promising to add $5.5 billion in school's operating aid over four years. Yet in 2009, after two years of more equitable funding, the state froze school aid, citing the financial crisis.
>
> (Joseph, 2015, p. 2)

Further cuts after the recession reduced funding to public schools by $9 billion and rerouted that funding to the state's general fund. Consequently, many school districts are close to going bankrupt (McDermott, 2015). Therefore, if the schools are "failing," and even by Cuomo's own count only a tiny fraction are, they are failing because they have been on austerity budgets for the last seven years while politicians have raked in millions (Marcou-O'Malley, 2014).

These funding cuts could have been avoided and school aid restored were it not for the austerity budget imposed by the governor. Joseph (2015) details how the cuts in education funding are in response to the lobbying efforts and political contributions from nine billionaire hedge fund managers. The different lobby groups I describe below who are funding Cuomo have interconnected boards and funders. In fact, Joseph (2015) reports on a March 2015 meeting of hedge fund managers titled "Bonds and Blackboards: Investing in Charter Schools" at the Harvard Club in New York City. The meeting, sponsored by the Gates and Walton Foundations, focused on how hedge fund managers could profit from the privatization of public schools.

Over the last decade, hedge fund managers have influenced education policy in New York by contributing more than $40 million to New York legislators and politicians (Gonzalez, 2015), including $4.8 million to Cuomo. In addition, contributions come from numerous groups promoting privatization and the corporate reform agenda. Some of these groups, including Education Reform Now, Students First NY, Families for Excellent Schools, and NY for a Balanced Albany, have interlocking boards and shift funds between each another.

During the most recent election, groups supporting privatizing and corporatizing education have funded business-friendly Republicans in the State Senate to counter the Democratically controlled Assembly. Cuomo also supported the election of the same Republicans, even though he had promised the Working Families Party that he would work to regain the Senate from Republicans if they did not support his primary challenger Zephyr Teachout. Teachout (Teachout & Kahn, 2014) is a progressive Fordham law professor who strongly challenged Cuomo's attack on teachers, public school, and unions. However, once the Working Families Party endorsed him, he reneged on his promise. It was these same Republicans who were crucial in getting Cuomo's April 1, 2015, proposal passed over the resistance of progressive Democrats in the Senate (Ravitch, 2015d).

The Impact of State and Federal Policies and Programs on Schools

As described earlier, in the mid-1990s, the state Board of Regents implemented a graduation requirement that students in New York State must pass five standardized exams. Not every school embraced this change. For example, the 28 schools that then made up the Performance Assessment Consortium and, in the late 1980s, had been granted a waiver from standardized testing, appealed the new testing requirements. After ten years of protesting, including suing the Commissioner three times, the consortium largely won the battle. However, for the remainder of the state's secondary schools, students are now required to pass the exams, making graduation more difficult for students from underfunded urban districts, students who are English Language Learners, and students with disabilities.

In 2002, President Bush signed NCLB into law after it passed with large majorities in both the Senate (87–10) and the House (381–41). The most prominent feature was the requirement that students in grades 3–8 would take standardized exams in reading (not language arts) and math. To ensure that attention would be paid to students of color and students with disabilities, NCLB required that students' scores be disaggregated by race, ethnic group, and ability/disability and that if any one group failed to make Adequate Yearly Progress (AYP), schools would be held accountable. Schools failing to make AYP faced a cascading increase in penalties, ranging from providing more professional development to replacing all the staff to closing the school and reopening it as a charter school.

However, as described earlier, the test score results are constantly manipulated to increase or decrease passing rates on particular tests depending on what is politically advantageous. Consequently, there is no validity in the passing rates;

they provide no information whether students are or are not improving from year to year. Furthermore, under NCLB, every state, with the approval of the federal Department of Education, determines for every test what knowledge and skills students need in order to demonstrate proficiency. States can, therefore, make achieving proficiency more or less difficult. However, for all states and every school, all students (regardless of ability or proficiency in the English language) are required to achieve proficiency by the year 2014.

Not only are the test scores worse than useless, AYP tells us little about whether a school is improving. Contrary to a common-sense interpretation of AYP, schools are not evaluated on whether their test scores are improving but, instead, whether their aggregated and disaggregated test scores exceed a minimum yearly threshold that gradually increases over the 12 years from 2002 to 2014 when a 100% passing rate is required. Consequently, a school is considered to be passing as long as its scores exceed the threshold, even if its scores fall. Similarly, schools that begin with initially low test scores may be considered failing even if they significantly improve their test scores, as long as those scores remain below the threshold. Therefore, achieving AYP may have nothing to do with whether a school's test scores rise or fall; achieving AYP depends only on exceeding the minimum threshold.

Because test scores strongly correlate with a student's family income, a school's score is more likely to reflect their students' average family income than the teaching or curriculum content. As a result, poor urban districts are likely to begin with low passing rates; even if their rates improve but do not exceed the minimum threshold, they will be designated as failing automatically. Alternatively, wealthier suburban districts, if their passing rates initially exceed the minimum threshold, may still be considered to be making progress even if their scores decline.

Moreover, because urban schools are likely to have a more diverse population than suburban schools, and each disaggregated demographic subgroup has to make progress or they all fail, urban schools have yet another reason to be classified as failing. Indeed, after the first year of NCLB, the largest percentage of failing schools in New York could be found in poor, urban school districts. Almost all (83%) of the failing schools were located in the big five urban districts: New York City, Buffalo, Rochester, Syracuse, and Yonkers (NYSSBA, 2003). Most of the remaining failing schools were in smaller urban districts. The failure rate among schools in large urban districts was and continues to be high, particularly at the middle school level. In Rochester, for example, all the middle schools failed in 2003, which led the superintendent to convert all the middle schools into grade 7–12 schools, temporarily averting penalties for failing to meet AYP by technically starting a new school. Since then, the middle schools have been reorganized every several years as a way of restarting the penalty clock.

In August 2010, the state of New York "won" RTTT funding. RTTT upped the ante by requiring that 20% of teachers' evaluations include not only students' scores on standardized tests but also how much their score improved from the beginning of the year to the end, also known as a Value Added Measure (VAM), a measure that has been thoroughly debunked as useful (Haertel, 2013). This resulted in such pedagogically inappropriate practices as teachers administering their final exams during the first week of class so that they could obtain baseline scores to compare with the students' scores when they retook the final exam at the end of the academic year. Teachers reported that students were often frustrated and confused by taking a test on content that they had not been taught. Even though there were no potential negative consequences for the students because of a two-year moratorium on using the scores to evaluate students, the concept that they were taking a test for which the scores were only relevant to the teacher was not easy for students to grasp. When some teachers tried to reassure the students that the tests would be used to evaluate not the students but the teachers, some students became distraught that their performance on a test might negatively impact their teachers. For teachers who do not give standardized exams—such as primary grade teachers and art, music, and gym teachers—the testing requirement led to all sorts of odd arrangements, such as evaluating primary grade art teachers based on the students' language arts scores in third grade.

However, the agreement that students' scores on standardized tests would compose only 20% of the teachers' evaluations was soon broken when in May 2011, "the Commissioner of Education, Dr. John King and Gov. Andrew M. Cuomo rammed a measure through the Board of Regents making state tests worth up to 40 percent of teacher evaluation" (Winerip, 2012, A-15). In response to criticism that too much weight would be given to test scores, the chancellor of the Board of Regents, Merryl Tisch, stated: "These are not perfect tools by any means. But that being said, I believe it is important to have an objective system to evaluate teachers on a professional basis. This is the beginning of such a process" (Otterman, 2011).

In response to the increase from 20% to 40%, the teachers' unions went to court and succeeded in temporarily blocking King and Cuomo. But Cuomo and Bloomberg wanted 40% of the assessment based on state and local test scores, and Cuomo threatened that if an agreement was not reached by February 16, 2012, he would unilaterally impose his own approach to measuring the quality of teachers' work. On that date, Cuomo and the unions reached an agreement in which testing would be used as 40% of teachers' evaluations, with teachers potentially having input on which tests might be used.

Following the agreement, schools began designing and incorporating what is known as an Annual Professional Performance Review (APPR) to assess every teacher based on the increase in their students' scores (VAM) on standardized tests and by two observations from two school administrators or an administrator and teacher (New York State Department of Education, 2012a) who are trained in the evaluation process.

The evaluation system, as I have described in depth in *Raising the Stakes: High-Stakes Testing and the Attack on Public Education in New York* (2013), is designed to portray teachers as failing. As NYSED admitted, the evaluation system was meant to classify a majority of teachers as "ineffective" or "developing." According to the State Education Department's "Guidance on New York State's Professional Performance Review Law and Regulations," (2012b) fewer than half the teachers should be rated as "effective" or "very effective," with most rated as "ineffective" and "developing." This will occur for two reasons. First, teachers are required to be rated on a bell curve so that 10% of teachers, whether based on test scores, observation, or other locally created criteria, must be rated as "ineffective" and 40% as "developing." Second, "before a teacher can be considered effective, her students' score growth must exceed the average for all teachers—that means based on scores, more than 50 percent of all teachers will not be effective" (Strauss, 2011, p. 1). Third, although the median total score will be 50 out of 100 points on the bell curve, teachers will have to score a total of 75 points or more to be rated "effective." Therefore, most teachers will be found to be "ineffective" or "developing." In New York City, if teachers are found to be "ineffective overall" for two consecutive years, the district can begin the process of removing the teacher (Ravitch, 2012).

Furthermore, the scoring rubric makes it possible for a teacher to be rated as "effective" in all the categories, from students' standardized test scores and administrator observations, and still not score enough points to receive an overall score of "effective" and, instead, be scored as "developing." This is comparable to passing all your tests in a course and then being informed that you failed the course overall.

Similarly, a teacher who receives a low rating because his or her students score poorly on the state exams, perhaps because they are English Language Learners or have learning disabilities, but then score "highly effective" on the nontest score criteria could be found to be "ineffective overall" (Strauss, 2012). This is an intended outcome of the policy that states: "Teachers rated ineffective on student performance based on objective assessments must be rated ineffective overall" (New York State Department of Education, 2012b).

However, as should be abundantly clear by now, the tests are neither objective nor accurate. Further, the scoring guide assumes that teachers in a school or district are naturally distributed along a continuum from ineffective to very effective and that some need to be fired. Moreover, districts were required to very quickly develop assessments for every subject in every grade; if the State Commissioner of Education John King did not find them sufficiently rigorous, he had the unilateral power to reject them (Ravitch, 2012, p. 3).

Outside of New York City, teachers' ratings are available to parents. While there was some concern from teachers and administrators that parents would use the ratings to decide what class they would like their child in, Carol Burris, award-winning and vocal superintendent, writes in Strauss' blog that as it turns out very few parents ever ask for them (Strauss, 2015). However, the New York City media, urged on by Bloomberg, won the right to publish the names and ratings of principals and third through eighth grade teachers of math and reading (the only subjects for which standardized tests already exist), which occurred on February 24, 2012. The New York City teachers' union, teachers, and educational experts have criticized how the evaluations are constructed and the release of individual teacher evaluations, but the process will continue. Ravitch (2012) succinctly summed up evaluating teachers based on their students' test scores and the grading curves by stating: "this is madness" (p. 5).

Nevertheless, many fewer teachers failed than would have been expected from the above: in 2014, about 90% of the teachers were rated as effective or very effective, with only 10% developing and 1% ineffective (Bakeman, 2015a), which led Governor Cuomo to describe the ratings as "baloney" (New York Times Editorial Board, 2015; Taylor, 2015b). Why my prediction and that of the SED of a high failure rate were not fulfilled is not hard to figure out. School districts are unlikely to feel that more than half of their teachers are ineffective or developing; if so, they would not have hired them. Furthermore, teachers found to be developing or ineffective have to be provided with professional development plans; given that RTTT has already imposed significant increases in expenses, most of which districts are not reimbursed for, school districts were not interested in taking on additional expenses and programs. Based on numerous reports to me from teachers and administrators, administrators simply figured out ways to increase the passing rates (based on reports from Bill Cala, superintendent of the Fairport public schools and former superintendent of the Rochester City School District, and other administrators).

Cuomo's now blatant attack on public schools, teachers, and unions has been building steadily over the last year. In this chapter, I highlight three events that reflect his increasing support for charter schools and denigration of the public schools. These events include his convening and participating in a three-day retreat in May 2014 on educational reform called "Camp Philos"; his speaking, in October, just ten days before election day, at an Albany rally promoting charter schools (Lovett, 2014); and his January 2015 State of the State speech (Blain & Lovett, 2015). These attacks have culminated in what Bill Cala calls "a war on teachers" (Taylor, 2015a) and "an all-out assault on public education, teachers, children, families, and local control" (Cala, 2015, p. 1). After describing those events, I will situate them within the governor's efforts to privatize education and diminish the power of teachers' unions. Lastly, I will show how Cuomo's efforts reflect the neoliberal/market fundamentalist agenda and are part of a concerted effort to privatize and profit from education.

Cuomo's Support for Corporate Reform

In the summer of 2014, Cuomo collaborated with antipublic school groups to plan a three-day retreat on educational reform called "Camp Philos" at White-face Lodge in the Adirondack Mountains. Education Reform Now (ERN), a nonprofit advocacy group that lobbies state and federal public officials to support charter schools, evaluate teachers based on students' scores on standardized tests, and eliminate teacher tenure, organized the retreat. ERN is a "sister entity" to Democrats for Education Reform (DFER). Both groups share an executive director, agenda, and funding from hedge fund managers. ERN and DFER are both funded by numerous foundations that support the neoliberal agenda, such as the Broad Foundation, the Walton Foundation, and the Arnold Foundation, to name a few (Schneider, 2014, 278–9.)

A significant percentage of those invited included hedge fund managers who see charter schools, because of government tax credits and other benefits, as an investment opportunity. No educators were invited. Admission to the retreat cost $1,000 per person, an amount that corporate executives, but few teachers, can afford. However, even when a few teachers submitted registrations, their registrations were returned. No educators allowed.

As news of the upcoming event spread, teachers, parents, students, members of the Alliance for Quality Education (AQE), and others decided to organize a protest at the lodge: what the New York State teachers' union dubbed "Picket in the Pines." Billy Easton, AQE's executive director stated that:

> The fact the Governor Cuomo is headlining this retreat is another clear sign that he has abandoned our public schools to fully embrace a testing and privatization agenda being pushed by the Wall Street types who are financing Camp Philos. Governor Cuomo says money does not matter to our public schools, but he is headlining this event to cash in on donations for this campaign that were rewards to give more money to privately run charter schools.
>
> (WNBZ news, 2014)

The adverse publicity generated by the picketing, one might guess, helped persuade Cuomo not to appear in person at Camp Philos but, instead, to present remotely.

Four months later, just two weeks before the election, at an Albany rally organized by charter school operators, promoters, and investors, Cuomo vowed to "break what is in essence one of the only remaining the public monopolies" (Lovett, 2014) and attacked the teachers' union for, he claimed, putting their own interests above those of children.

Cuomo's criticism of public education and support for privatization contributed to the New York State United Teachers not endorsing Cuomo for governor in the Democratic primary where Cuomo faced a challenge from Zephyr Teachout and Tim Wu. Teachout is a law professor at Fordham University whose challenge of Cuomo was her first campaign for public office. The educational platform of Teachout and her lieutenant governor, Tim Wu, was the exact opposite of Cuomo's. Their seven priorities included: full and equal funding for public education, ending high-stakes testing, ending privatization, empowering local communities, suspending the school to prison pipeline, halting Common Core, and prioritizing early intervention (http://www.teachoutwu.com/education). The public, evidently, was so dissatisfied with Cuomo that, with little funding and name recognition, Teachout received 34.3% of the vote (New York Times, 2014).

Snubbed, Cuomo, in a press conference previous to his January 2015 State of the State speech, increased his attack the public schools, teachers, and unions (Saratogian New York, 2015). Cuomo, in the words of the president of the New York State United Teachers, Karen Magee, "declared a war on the public schools" (Taylor, 2015). He said that public education "probably has been the single greatest failure of the state" (sic) (Dewitt, 2015) and, in response, proposed changing teacher evaluation and tenure. He claimed that the reforms will improve the teaching profession by aiding in recruiting top candidates and raising standards, but his proposals are likely to have the opposite effect. Because teaching as a career will become much more uncertain, potential candidates will be discouraged from considering teaching. Further, he increased his support for charter schools, proposing to raise the limit on the number of charter schools from 460 to 600 and diverting more state funding to charter, private, and parochial schools.

He aimed to improve teaching by increasing the percentage of teachers who will be designated as "developing" or "ineffective" so that "weak teachers" can be fired and by linking eligibility for tenure to those ratings. Further, he desired to make it much more difficult to earn a rating of effective or very effective.

As described earlier, he proposed increasing the significance of standardized tests scores in evaluating teachers. Currently, as part of an agreement in applying for and "winning" Race to the Top funding, 40% of teachers' evaluations are based on their students' scores on standardized exams. He criticized the current teacher evaluation process for rating too few teachers as ineffective, and, therefore, the results were "not real" (Taylor, 2014). He argued that because, in 2014, (Bakeman, 2015a) only 35% of New York's students scored at the proficiency level on the Common Core reading exam and only 39% on the math exam (Taylor, 2015), the low percentage of teachers found to be "developing" or "ineffective" is "baloney" (New York Times Editorial Board, 2015, A-26).

However, as I described, the State Department of Education has for the last several decades manipulated the test scores for political purposes, and the same has continued for the Common Core exams. The passing rate was determined before the tests were given and set at a level to portray the schools and teachers as failing. In a sense, Cuomo is correct. The results are "not real," not because teachers' ratings are too high but because the students' scores are too low.

That the passing rate was set too low was acknowledged by the state regents and legislature when they agreed that the scores could not be used for two years as a high-stakes assessment for students (i.e., to determine graduation). A year earlier, Cuomo had proposed to the legislature a bill giving the same two-year protection to teachers and administrators, which the legislature passed and he praised but in the fall of 2014 ultimately vetoed (Decker, 2014; Seller, 2014).

Instead, Cuomo decided to make the assessment process even higher stakes for teachers and to increase the percentage of teachers who are found ineffective or failing; if teachers receive that rating for two consecutive years, they can be fired. Cuomo proposed increasing to 50% the significance of students' scores on standardized exams in teacher evaluations. Further, so that school districts cannot reduce the impact of low scores on a teacher's evaluation by assigning high observation scores, he proposed that "we will set the scoring band for both the student growth measure and the observation portion of the scores at the state level" (Governor's Office, 2015, p. 2). It is unclear who the "we" is, how they will be selected, or how they will be compensated. Furthermore, "if a teacher is rated ineffective on either portion of the score [students' test scores or professional observations], he or she cannot receive a rating of Effective or Highly Effective, but rather Developing or Ineffective" (Governor's Office, 2015, p. 2).

Moreover, not only will it be much more difficult to be rated as an effective teacher but also the importance of such a rating increases as Cuomo proposed that, "tenure will only be granted when a teacher achieves five consecutive years of effective ratings" (Governor's Office, 2015, p. 3). This will make it close to impossible for many teachers to become eligible for tenure as students' test scores rise and fall significantly from year to year and, therefore, that one-year rating as "developing" becomes highly probable.

The proposed system is harmful to students who are differently abled or from low- or even high-income families. Because the scores of students with disabilities or students in honors programs may not increase much over the year, teachers will be hesitant to teach students who do not achieve the testing gains necessary to achieve a rating of effective.

Another requirement for "winning" Race to the Top funding was raising the cap on the number of charter schools permitted in the state, which the state did by increasing the number from 200 to 460. According to the New York City Department of Education, 210 charter schools are planning to operate in the city in the 2015–2016 school year (New York City Department of Education, 2015). Cuomo has expressed his concern that the number of charter schools operating in New York City is nearing its limit and, therefore, wants to raise by 100 the cap on the state as a whole and remove New York City as a subcategory so that the number of charter schools allowed in New York City only counts toward a new total of 600.

Cuomo's support for charter schools was also reflected in his previous proposal to use state funds to supplement funding for charter schools. He had already intervened in New York City's regulations regarding charter schools by giving charter schools priority regarding space in public schools, including whole buildings. This regulation has forced public schools to operate with less space in their own buildings and, in some cases, to search for space or move to other buildings. In one case, a New York City has had to pay $11,000 a year per student in rent for the Success Academy Charter Schools, bringing the cost to the city to more than $24,000 per year per student (Chapman, 2014).

In his State of the State speech, Cuomo proposed a "$100 million tax credit for public and private scholarships" by creating the Education Tax Credit that will allow "taxpayers to claim [a 75%] tax credit for eligible contributions to public schools, school improvement organizations, local education funds and educational scholarship organizations" (New York State (2005, February 20). Education: The great equalizer. https://www.ny.gov/2015-opportunity-agenda/education-great-equalizer-0). The phrase "education scholarship organizations" indicates that the proposal attempts to circumvent New York State's legal prohibitions against vouchers to fund students' private school education. In the words of the press release, Cuomo desires "to support private investments from individuals and businesses in educational programs that support choices for their students." While the bill also mentions public schools along with charter schools, it is clear that the proposal is in response to the hedge fund managers and other wealthy individuals who want to benefit by investing in charter schools.

Cuomo's proposals, then, are intended to make it more difficult for teachers to receive ratings of effective or very effective, for teachers to earn tenure, and to increase the funding for and number of charter schools in order to end "the public school monopoly." He has also disparaged public schools teachers by claiming that they are only interested in advancing their own careers.

Cuomo's Neoliberal Allies

At first, Cuomo's attack on public education and teachers' unions may seem difficult to explain given that, first, he is an elected public official who you might think would support the public services and education that the state provides and, second, he is a member of the Democratic Party, the party of Franklin D. Roosevelt and Lyndon Johnson, which, at its best, promoted equality and social democracy. Instead, he has adopted a neoliberal ideology and discourse condemning public schools and other nonmarket approaches (Randolph, 2014).

Cuomo has worked closely with hedge fund managers and other advocates of privatization, as reflected in his collaboration with the Democrats for Education Reform (DFER) and Education Reform Now (ERN) in planning the events to promote school privatization at "Camp Philos." Cuomo has benefitted financially from his relationship with hedge fund managers and other investors by advocating neoliberal reforms. DFER and ERN are self-described sister organizations with a significant number of hedge fund managers on their boards (Schneider, 2014, p. 279). Schneider cites DFER's Statement of Purpose stating that they "believe that reforming broken public school systems . . . through bold and revolutionary leadership. . . . Opening up the traditional top-down monopoly" (Democrats for Education Reform, n.d.). Both organizations, then, spread the falsehood that our schools are failing because they are monopolies and can only be improved through market competition. Both organizations see issues such as reducing poverty as issues to be ignored.

Cuomo, like DFER and ERN, builds directly on the neoliberal ideas first promulgated in the 1950s by the Nobel Prize-winning economist Milton Friedman, whose writing on economics is probably the most well known in the United States. His book, *Free to Choose* (Friedman & Friedman, 1990), coauthored with his wife Rose, was a best-selling paperback and was made into a television series. Friedman's ideas were disseminated by his colleagues and students at the University of Chicago and are reiterated by politicians, economists, and popular writers. Friedman desired to eliminate public schools and was an early proponent of referring to public schools as "government schools." In *Public Schools: Make Them Private* (1995), Friedman promoted restructuring education "by enabling a private, for-profit industry to develop that will provide a wide variety of learning opportunities and offer effective competition to public schools" (p. 1).

Neoliberals have taken up Friedman's language in referring to schools as "government monopolies," including on Fox News (Stossel, 2013) and by Jonah Goldberg, the syndicated columnist and author of the best-selling *Liberal Fascism: The Secret History of the Left, From Mussolini to the Politics of Meaning* (2008). Goldberg (2007) cites Friedman, stating that:

> Friedman noted long ago that the government is bad at providing services—
> that's why he wanted public schools to be called "government schools." . . .
> One of the surest ways to leave a kid "behind" is to hand him over to the
> government. Americans want universal education, just as they want univer-
> sally safe food. But nobody believes that the government should run all the
> restaurants, farms and supermarkets. Why should it run the vast majority of
> schools—particularly when it gets terrible results?
>
> (12-A)

The attack on public schools, notes Johnson and Salle (2004), is:

> [A]imed not only at the public schools but at a broader range of progres-
> sive values and policies. It must be understood as a part of a multi-front
> ideological campaign that the Right has pursued very aggressively, and so
> far quite successfully, against the idea that government should be in the
> business of helping people.
>
> (p. 4)

Cuomo also echoes those who attack not only public schools but also unions in general and teachers' unions in particular. Johnson and Salle (2004) cite many examples of the neoliberal and neoconservative attack on teachers' unions, including this from Charlene Haar in *Special Interests in the Classroom*:

> The strongest players in the schoolhouse game are the two teachers' unions,
> the National Education Association (NEA) and the American Federation
> of Teachers (AFT). . . . Increasing the welfare state, not improving chil-
> dren's education, is uppermost on this [NEA and AFT] agenda. . . . Despite

their rhetoric, the NEA and AFT routinely sabotage efforts for meaningful reform. . . . The NEA and AFT are merely protecting themselves at the expense of children.

(Haar, 1996, p. 37)

The corporate reformers aspire to control the discourse of public education, portraying themselves and their reform agenda as the only one that aims to improve education for all students, particularly for children living in our urban areas. While Cuomo ignores the more intractable issues of school segregation and child poverty, he claims that he is supporting charter schools because "education is not about the districts and not about the pensions and not about the unions, and not about the lobbyists and not about the PR firms—education is about the students, and the students come first" (Cuomo, 2014).

Perhaps surprisingly (or not), given his silence on New York's status as the state with the most segregated schools, at a 2012 observance commemorating Dr. Martin Luther King, Jr.'s birthday, Cuomo cited the 1954 Brown v. Board of Education ruling, lamenting that because of failing public schools, "the great equalizer that was supposed to be the public education system can now be the great discriminator" (Kaplan & Taylor, 2012). Perhaps he has forgotten that the Supreme Court case declared that children cannot overcome the harm caused by segregated schools and, therefore, desegregation should come first. Instead, he portrayed teachers' unions as special interests and teachers as only caring about their pensions and contracts, while only he and others like him are "for the children."

Cuomo and other corporate reformers ignore data that shows that New York's public schools are highly racially and economically segregated; indeed, New York has separate and unequal schools. A new study by The Civil Rights Project at UCLA (Kucsera, 2014) confirms what many of us always suspected: New York State has the most segregated schools in the United States. Sixty years after Brown versus Board of Education supposedly ended segregation, New York's schools are more segregated than in the past. In 2009, writes Kucsera, "black and Latino students in the state had the highest concentration in intensely-segregated public schools (less than 10% white enrollment), the lowest exposure to white students, and the most uneven distribution with white students across schools" (p. 1).

Rochester has the fifth highest poverty rate of *all* the cities in the United States and the second highest of mid-sized cities. Ninety percent of the students in the Rochester City School District come from families who live in economic poverty. Yet Cuomo, who regularly makes public announcements on many issues, from urging us to shop locally for Easter presents to how to avoid ticks while hiking, has remained silent on the issue of segregation (Bryant, 2014).

Cuomo accuses teachers of being only for their own interests and not the interests of children and, therefore, of having special interests. As irrational as this sounds, it is even more ridiculous when you consider how responsive he is to the desires of CEOs and their investors, including hedge fund managers. This is not surprising, given that he received $400,000 for his reelection campaign from one charter school operator and another $400,000 this year from bankers, hedge fund managers, real estate executives, philanthropists, and advocacy groups who have flocked to charter schools and other privatization efforts (Anderson, 2014).

Moreover, by pushing for education reform, Cuomo may be providing an excuse to either reduce or hold education funding steady when schools are still recovering from deep cuts during the recent recession and the state is under a court order to increase funding of urban districts (Education Law Center, 2015). In his State of the State address, Cuomo threatened that he would increase elementary and secondary education funding by only "1.7 percent, as pursuant to the existing formula," unless the legislature puts all of his reform proposals in place, which would result in him approving a 4.8% increase (Connor, 2015, p. 7).

Cuomo coerced the legislature to pass his education proposals by embedding the proposals in his annual budget. He has repeatedly touted the fact that as governor, the legislature has produced and he has signed four on-time budgets, which are due on April 1st. By submitting it only days before the April 1st deadline, he limited the discussion on education proposal and coerced the legislature into passing the bill on time with few modifications.

It should be clear that Cuomo is not interested in the children but rather in the wealthy hedge fund managers and charter school CEOS who contributed to his reelection campaign and who he wants on board for his next campaign, whether it is for reelection as governor of New York or for election as president of the United States. Joseph (2015), in a recent exposé, revealed the interconnections between Cuomo, charter school CEOs, hedge fund managers, and educators such as Joel Klein, when he was chancellor of the New York City Schools.

Cuomo, as an attorney general and a governor, has benefitted from individual contributions from hedge fund managers totaling $4.83 million. Moreover, he has benefitted from $2.53 million in contributions to the New York State Democratic Party Committee's Housekeeping Fund, which Hedge Clippers, a group investigating the impact of hedge fund managers on state education and economic policies, describes as "a Cuomo controlled slush fund that has been used to pay for advertisements to support the governor" (Joseph, 2015). Hedge Clippers is a new organization backed by the American Federation of Teachers, Zephyr Teachout, and labor and community organizations. Bellafante describes Hedge Clippers as aiming at:

> [O]utlining the ways hedge funds bleed the economy through self-interested practice and then extend the damage through the lavish purchase of political influence. According to an analysis by the group, hedge fund managers have made $40 million in political contributions in New York State over the last 15 years.
>
> (Bellafante, 2015, p. 24)

Furthermore, as Teachout and Wu (2014) describe, hedge fund managers financed a takeover of the New York State Senate by funding, for $4.3 million, a new Political Action Committee (or PAC) named New Yorkers for a Balanced Albany that would elect enough Republican Senators to gain control over the Senate and, in cooperation with Cuomo, push through legislation that would favor charter schools. The Senate Republicans are very much against increasing state school aid for education. According to Teachout and Wu (2014), the Senate Education Committee Chairman, Republican John Flanagan, said "that new funding should prioritize the needs of wealthy and middle class districts rather than prioritizing high needs districts." (Bakeman, 2014, cited in Teachout and Wu, 2014, p. 16).

Just one of the ways during the last budget negotiations in which the contributing hedge fund managers benefitted from their political contributions was the defeat of legislative efforts to support scholarships to undocumented college students, raising the minimum wage, and property tax relief for middle-class homeowners. Instead, the budget that was passed includes a sales tax exemption for yachts that cost more than $230,000, which will save the new owners a minimum of $20,000 (Craig, 2015).

As implied above, a second benefit for Cuomo and his wealthy funders is that in calling for teacher evaluations, school reform, and more charter schools, attention is diverted from efforts to solve real problems. Cuomo is engaged in what Ravitch calls a "purposeful distraction" (2014). Instead of devoting time to debate the pros and cons of college scholarships or raising the minimum wage, attention is paid to Cuomo's education reform proposals.

The Rising Public Resistance to the Neoliberal Project

While the State Department of Education, Commissioner King, Chancellor Tisch, and Governor Cuomo have the backing of state and federal laws and millions of dollars in funding from the Gates, Walton, and other foundations and hedge fund managers, parents, teachers, and students have organized mounting resistance. The public is increasingly aware that education policy is made by politicians, wealthy heads of foundations (for example, Gates, Walton, Broad), corporations (Pearson), and hedge fund managers. In the remainder of this chapter, I describe that mounting resistance and the results of Cuomo's education reform policies.

Thousands of parents and teachers spoke up when the commissioner of education embarked on what he initially dubbed a "listening tour" of the state to hear concerns from parents about the Common Core State Standards, the curriculum, and assessments. However, in the first few meetings, King spoke more than his listened, lecturing the parents on their responsibility. The audiences grew hostile in response, and King initially canceled the hearings only to reschedule them when it became apparent that he could not ignore the public. Subsequently, hearings were held across the state.

In the Rochester area, the hearing was scheduled for a Wednesday afternoon at a local high school. Approximately 650 teachers, parents, and community members showed up; those who wanted to provide three minutes of testimony were assigned a number for when they would speak. During the first three hours, dozens of people spoke against the Common Core Standards, curriculum, and tests. Only one person spoke in favor of the Common Core, a superintendent of a local suburban district. Otherwise, everyone that spoke was critical of the standards themselves and the New York Engage curriculum, which the SED developed and strongly suggested that teachers use if they hoped to prepare their students for the standardized exams.

The exams and the curriculum were often described as developmentally inappropriate, the New York Engage curriculum as too scripted, and the exams themselves as too time consuming (NYC Public School Parents, 2012). Furthermore, teachers had to sign a "gag order" that promised that they would not look at the questions on the exam and, if they did, that they would not share what they read with anyone. If they did, they could be disciplined, including losing their jobs (Sawchuk, 2014).

Commissioner King and Chancellor Tisch continued to defend the standards, exams, and curriculum. In the end, the only concession that they made was not to use the results from the first two years as high-stakes exams for the students, that is, as a criterion for graduation. However, it could and will be used as a high-stake test in the evaluation of teachers. Furthermore, the low scores have been used, as stated, as a bludgeon to attack teachers, so they have certainly been high stakes as Cuomo and advocates of privatization have used the low passing rates in urban areas to push for charter schools.

Still, numerous organizations have pushed back, and new ones have been created. One new organization created in the summer of 2013 is the New York State Allies for Public Education (NYSAPE) (http://www.nysape.org) representing 57 local organizations—including Rochester's Coalition for Justice in Education, Southern Tier Parents Against Common Core, Opt Out Ithaca, Pencils Down Rockland County, Class Size Matters, and Reclaiming Our Public Schools— and five statewide organizations, including Time Out From Testing and NY Stop Grad High Stakes Tests.

In NYSAPE's most recent press release from March 13, 2015, they describe how thousands of New Yorkers have come together in support of public education by attending rallies and forums across the state. On their website, they list *40* forums (italics added) scheduled across that state during the month of March, which is the month before the legislature would act on Cuomo's education reform proposals. The forums attracted large crowds. In the Rochester area, the forum held in the suburban Fairport home of vocal critic Bill Cala (2015) attracted 1,500 people. The forum organized by teachers in Spencerport, a conservative suburban community, attracted 650 people. A forum organized by parents in Pittsford, a wealthy suburb, had 450 people in a room that had a capacity of 300, and many were turned away. Forums scheduled for April struggled to find venues with sufficient capacity.

Teachers have been increasingly active in pushing back, although the media often describes teachers, omitting parents, as the only group resisting Cuomo's proposals (New York State Allies for Public Education, 2015a, 2015b). On March 30, 2015, the New York State United Teachers President Karen Magee called for parents to opt their children out of the Common Core exams (Karlin, 2015). Moreover, 88 teacher associations endorsed strong resolutions against high-stakes testing (Ravitch, 2015b).

Not only are teachers and parents protesting but also the New York Council of School Superintendents and the New York School Boards Association. These organizations issued a joint statement opposing Cuomo's proposal to change teacher evaluation. They point out that the proposal just passed is the fourth change to the teacher evaluation system in five years. Additionally, nearly 100 school district superintendents have signed a petition to save public education in New York (Ravitch, 2015a).

All the grassroots political activity critiquing Cuomo's education policies contributed to a steep decline in Cuomo's approval ratings with the public. As the Quinnipiac Poll headline stated: "Cuomo drops to lowest score ever . . . Governor losing school battle to teachers' unions" (Carroll, 2015). The survey revealed a drop in his job approval rating from 58% to 50%, his lowest rating during this governorship. However, it seems that the only rating Cuomo cares about is his rating with the billionaire hedge fund managers.

The Current Status of Corporate Reform in New York

Cuomo showed that he is both smart and ruthless. By pitting the Republicans in the Senate against the Democrats in the Assembly, on April 1, 2015, he got the votes he needed and most of the reforms he wanted.

The legislators made slight revisions to his proposals and separated some of Cuomo's proposals out of the budget to be reconsidered on their own later in the spring, including raising the limit on the number of charter schools in the state and the 75% tax credit for donating to a charter school or to a private school "scholarship fund."

Here are the issues with a description of the key points in the final law adapted from a summary by Bakeman (2015b). I describe them in depth because they significantly transform public education and have draconian consequences on public schools and public teachers. Furthermore, they exemplify the lack of trust of teachers, administrators, and even the public.

Teacher Evaluations

Cuomo called the current teacher evaluations "baloney" because he felt that, given only slightly more than 30% of students scored at the level of proficiency, too many teachers were rated as effective or highly effective. Therefore, he wanted to increase the significance of the results of the scores on the standardized tests to 50% of teachers' evaluations, and he wanted to make it impossible for a teacher whose students scored low on the standardized tests to be effective or highly effective. Lastly, he wanted to remove the teacher observation component of the assessment from administrators in their own school to administrators in other schools or, if their district only had one elementary or secondary, an administrator from another district. Many suburban districts have only one secondary school, and many rural districts have only one of elementary, middle, or secondary school. Requiring observations by administrators from another district will impose significant hardships on many districts. Cuomo essentially got what he wanted. He got everything he wanted. The new state law requires that teacher evaluations be:

> [B]ased on student performance on state exams that includes a mandatory state test and an optional one. . . . Teachers won't be evaluated based on students' absolute performance; rather, the state will develop "growth scores" based on the exams that measure how much students improve from one year to the next. Teachers whose courses don't end in state exams will be evaluated based on "student learning objectives," or expectations of what students will learn in a year, which will be developed by the state.
>
> For the observation component of the evaluation, there will be two required observations and one optional one. The required observations will be performed by a principal or administrator and an "independent" evaluator, who can be a principal or administrator from another school within the district or another district.
>
> The state education department "shall determine the weights and scoring ranges" and "set parameters for appropriate targets for student growth" for the required and optional components and subcomponents of the rating system. However, there are certain rules prescribed in law that determine the overall scores that teachers can receive depending on their scores on the two components. For example, if teachers earn an "ineffective" rating based on student performance on the required state test, they may not earn "effective" or "highly effective" overall.
>
> If teachers use both the required and optional tests, and their combined score based on student performance on the tests is "ineffective," they must be rated "ineffective" overall. Teachers who are rated "ineffective" on the observation category may not get "effective" or "highly effective" ratings overall.

Districts may no longer consider the following in determining educators' evaluations: lesson plans, student portfolios (with some exceptions) and student or parent feedback surveys.

(Bakeman, 2015b)

The problems with this evaluation plan are many. First, we know that the standardized tests are an inaccurate measure of the students' learning and should not be used as a high-stakes evaluation of the students, teachers, school, or district. In fact, Regent Cashen sent Ravitch an e-mail to post on her blog the day after the proposal was approved, stating that she "cannot endorse the use of the current tests for teacher/principal evaluation since it was not the purpose for which they were developed." Numerous educational associations "have cautioned that student tests should not be used to evaluate teachers" (Ravitch, 2015c). Second, because not achieving a rating of effective or highly effective on any part of the evaluation automatically results in an overall rating of developing or ineffective for the teacher, rather than being averaged, this procedure will result in a higher failure rate. Essentially, any rating of ineffective on any part of the evaluation results in an overall rating of ineffective. Third, given that teachers will be observed by administrators who are not from their school, and the act contains regulations prohibiting the observer from using any of the usual artifacts that educators use to make sense of the quality of a teacher's work: lesson plans, portfolios, feedback from students or parents, or professional goal setting, the observer will have limited knowledge of the context in which the teacher teaches. In essence, the law assumes that a teacher can be evaluated merely by observing their classroom without any knowledge of the students in the classroom, what occurred in the past, or plans for the future.

Teacher Tenure

Under current law, teachers are eligible for tenure after three years of probationary teaching. In New York, tenure protects teachers from arbitrary dismissal by requiring that efforts to remove teachers follow due process. Cuomo had proposed that teachers would have a probationary period of five years and would be ineligible for tenure if they received a rating of ineffective or developing during *any* of those five years. This emphasis on test scores forces a teacher to lose eligibility for tenure if for any single year students on average scored below proficient. If the plan is implemented in the way that Cuomo hopes, most teachers would never earn tenure. Moreover, given how easy it is for teachers to be removed from their position, teaching would become a very precarious job.

The legislation as passed was only slightly amended:

Before teachers and principals may be offered tenure, they'll serve a probationary period of four years, instead of the current three years, and they must earn "effective" or "highly effective" ratings for three of the four years. Educators who earn an "ineffective" rating during the fourth year may not be offered tenure, but they may be offered an additional probationary year.

Teachers who have received tenure in another school district who weren't fired for poor performance will serve a three-year probationary period.

Educators may be fired at any time during their probationary periods.

(Bakeman, 2015b)

Given that the scores of students in any teacher's class can vary significantly from year to year, these new regulations will make it much more difficult for teachers to gain tenure. Further, once they gain tenure, they would be very hesitant to leave for another district given that they would forfeit tenure and endure a three-year probationary period. Such a draconian policy will significantly discourage people from entering the profession and reveals how little the governor and legislature value teaching as a profession.

Teacher Discipline

Teachers who are rated ineffective, which could result entirely from students' scores on standardized tests, can be easily dismissed with or without tenure, as in the two cases below. Also note that having students receive low test scores is described a "teacher discipline." In addition, in the first case, teachers, in their own defense, must provide "clear and convincing evidence" and, in the second, "mistaken identity." Lastly, teachers are provided minimal time for their defense. Teachers are presumed guilty. The text:

> Teachers or principals who earn two consecutive "ineffective" ratings may be brought up on charges of incompetence by their schools boards and would have to provide "clear and convincing evidence" in order to avoid being fired. The decision must be made within 90 days of the charges being initiated. Educators who earn three consecutive "ineffective" ratings must be brought up on charges of incompetence and could argue only "fraud" as a defense. "Fraud" includes mistaken identity. The decision must be made within 30 days.
>
> (Bakeman, 2015b)

So as to expedite the decision-making process, "disciplinary hearings will be conducted by a single hearing officer."

Receivership

The legislation requires that each year the state designate one of every 20 schools as failing and all that fail can potentially be turned over to a "non-profit entity, another school district, or an individual." In New York, the charter schools are technically nonprofit. The receiver has sole power to make any decision or policy, including removing all the teachers and administrators.

Schools that have persistently low test scores, which seem to be the only assessment tool, will be placed in receivership, which basically entails handing the school over to another school district, individual, or charter school. Given that there seems to be little incentive for another school district to take over the school, it seems that the likely outcome will be handing a school over to an individual or charter school. As is clear below, whoever is given the school has absolute authority to terminate any teaching, administrative, and staff positions and "may request" renegotiating collective bargaining agreements. However, given that the receiver has absolute control, it seems that any contract could be eliminated at any time.

I provide extensive detail below to document how detailed the regulations are and how easily public schools can be closed, disbanded, and turned over to a charter school or individual who would have absolute control over the school while the public, which funds the school, is marginalized.

> Schools whose performance falls in the lowest 5 percent in the state for three consecutive years will be designated "failing schools" under the budget. Schools with 10 years of low performance will be called "persistently failing schools."
>
> "Persistently failing schools" will have one year to implement "a comprehensive education plan . . . that includes rigorous performance metrics and goals," which has to be approved by the state. "Failing schools" will have two years.
>
> When the one-year or two-year periods expire, the education department will conduct a performance review of the schools. If the schools show "demonstrable improvement" based on their turnaround plans, they will remain under local control, and their performance will continue to be reviewed annually. If the schools do not improve, a receiver will be appointed for a period of no more than three years to "manage and operate all aspects of the school and to develop and implement a school intervention plan." The district has the ability to choose the receiver, subject to state approval. If a district does not choose a receiver within 60 days, the state appoints one.
>
> "The independent receiver may be a non-profit entity, another school district, or an individual," according to the bill's language. The receiver "shall have the power to supersede any decision, policy or regulation . . . that in the sole judgment of the receiver conflicts with the school intervention plan."
>
> The receiver will be able to "replace teachers and administrators" and "abolish the positions of all members of the teaching and administrative and supervisory staff assigned to the failing or persistently failing school

and terminate the employment of any building principal assigned to such a school, and require such staff members to reapply for their positions in the school if they so choose."

When teacher or principal positions are abolished, the current teachers or principals with the lowest rating on their most recent performance evaluations will be fired. Seniority will be considered in case of a tie.

When teachers and principals reapply for their jobs, a staffing committee will determine whether the applicants are qualified. "The receiver shall have full discretion regarding hiring decisions but must fill at least fifty percent of the newly defined positions with the most senior former school staff who are determined by the staffing committee to be qualified."

Those who are not rehired "shall not have any right to bump or displace any other person employed by the district, but shall be placed on a preferred eligibility list."

Here's what the bill says about collective bargaining when schools are under receivership: "In order to maximize the rapid achievement of students at the applicable school, the receiver may request that the collective bargaining unit or units representing teachers and administrators and the receiver, on behalf of the board of education, negotiate a receivership agreement that modifies the applicable collective bargaining agreement or agreements with respect to any failing schools in receivership."

"The receivership agreement may address the following subjects: the length of the school day; the length of the school year; professional development for teachers and administrators; class size; and changes to the programs, assignments, and teaching conditions in the school in receivership," the bill says. "The receivership agreement shall not provide for any reduction in compensation unless there shall also be a proportionate reduction in hours and shall provide for a proportionate increase in compensation where the length of the school day or school year is extended. The receivership agreement shall not alter the remaining terms of the existing/underlying collective bargaining agreement which shall remain in effect."

The receiver will be able to "order the conversion of a school in receivership that has been designated as failing or persistently failing . . . into a charter school."

The receiver will also be able to increase salaries of current or prospective teachers and administrators, extend the school day or year and add full-day kindergarten and pre-kindergarten classes, in the case of elementary schools.

The receiver will have the authority to reallocate resources within the school's existing budget and review proposed budgets before they're presented to voters for approval. The receiver will be a non-voting member of the school board.

(Bakeman, 2015a)

Teacher Preparation Programs

In New York, obtaining teacher certification entails satisfying the requirements of the edTPA program, which is a national certification administered by Pearson. In addition, the governor sought to impose further restrictions on persons wishing to enter teacher education programs or gain certification. As noted below, entering teacher certification programs required achieving a grade point average of 3.0, a quantitative rather than qualitative measure.

> The budget will establish new admission requirements for graduate schools of education in New York as well as scholarships for high-achieving students who attend graduate schools and commit to teaching in the state for five years.
>
> Graduate schools of education will be required to "adopt rigorous selection criteria geared to predicting a candidate's academic success in its program," including a cumulative 3.0 grade point average during an applicant's undergraduate career and a minimum score on the Graduate Record Examination or an equivalent entrance exam.
>
> Up to 15 percent of an incoming class may be exempted from the selection criteria "based on a student's demonstration of potential to positively contribute to the teaching profession or other extenuating circumstances."
>
> (Bakeman, 2015a)

For now, the corporate reformers have won. Cuomo has placed an even heavier emphasis on standardized tests, has made it almost impossible for teachers to gain tenure, and has constrained teaching so that it is hard to claim it is a profession.

I have provided the specific legislation resulting from Cuomo's education reform proposals because each excerpt demonstrates several aspects of the changes in governance under market fundamentalist social imaginaries.

First, local school districts have largely lost control over how their teachers and schools will be evaluated. Achieving tenure will depend to a significant degree on how students perform on the Common Core Standardized exams. Likewise, each year, schools that have scored in the lowest 5% for three consecutive years will begin the process of being placed in receivership, which includes being converted to a charter school or handed over to an individual. It matters little whether the district, parents, or students value the teacher or the school. The assumption on the part of the legislature is that learning can be objectively measured and that students' scores on *one test* can be the main piece of information to decide a teacher's career and the future of a school.

People, teaching, and learning are therefore reduced to numbers. Ball observes that:

> The examination is a mechanism of simultaneous evaluation and comparison. . . . The learner is made visible and calculable, but power is rendered

invisible ... In teaching, the articulation of performance and improvement in terms of student test scores ... linked to ... performance pay.

(Ball, 2015, p. 299)

Ravitch has observed that in New York, and perhaps in most states, teaching is the only profession so tightly regulated.

Second, while Cuomo did not increase the number of standardized tests, he has increased immensely their significance. Not only are they now worth 50% rather than 40% of the teachers' evaluation, students scoring in the bottom half—developing and ineffective—will result in their teachers losing the opportunity to achieve tenure and will risk getting fired. Teachers, parents, and students already attest to the pressure everyone feels regarding the tests. That pressure will be increased exponentially.

Third, parents, teachers, and administrators have had almost no impact on the legislative process. The governor, most legislators, the chancellor, the commissioner, and most but not all of the Board of Regents have dismissed the objections of educators and parents.

Moreover, the media have often poorly portrayed parents' objections to the tests. Cuomo claims that parents have only begun to object because the teachers have riled them up. Similarly, some of the press blames resistance to the tests on the teachers' unions. In response to the continuing parent-organized events to educate the public about the Common Core, Rochester's *Democrat and Chronicle* newspaper editorialized that parents who opt their children out of the tests are doing so because they claim:

> "Tests stress kids out." But these tests have no consequence on the child's grade or ability to advance, so that's not what is causing them to fret. ... Teachers have been whipped into a frenzy by union leaders who have lost their decades-long chokehold on state government, its citizens, and the education system. The unions are employing this tactic [opting out of tests] to fight politicians who may, or may not, have a clue how to truly educate a child—but know the union way doesn't work, especially in disaster zones like the City School District, where schools would lose funding if too many students opt out. Parents, before you opt out, know who you're really opting out for.
>
> (Editor, 2015, April 9)

The editor makes numerous errors. Contrary to the claims of Cuomo and Duncan, who I will talk about in the next chapter, parents can and are thinking for themselves. Parents realize that the tests have consequences for their children. The tests will make it difficult for their teachers to earn tenure, and many people, particularly ones who are creative and intelligent, will no longer consider teaching as a career. Further, their school could be closed and handed over to a charter school that is not required to hold public board meetings or even allow public visitors, or transferred to one individual who would have absolute power. Contrary to the editorial, losing your public school seems to be a consequence. The editor denigrates parents and teachers.

However, most parents whose children attend public schools and their teachers know that their schools are not failing and their teachers are not failures. Therefore, they have responded to Cuomo and the commissioner and chancellor by organizing hundreds of forums on the Common Core State Standards and communicating their dissatisfaction to the governor, legislators, commissioner, chancellor, and the regents. At recent hearings, many parents have concluded that they have no way to effect education policy except by opting their children out of tests. During the first week of the statewide Common Core exams in April, school districts reported high percentages of parents opting out their children, some ranging from 75% to 90% (Harris & Fesseden, 2015). New York State Allies for Public Education reported that as of April 23, 2015, 200,666 students have refused to take the ELS tests with 73% of districts reporting (New York State Allies for Public Education, 2015a; http://www.nysape.org/nysape-pr-parents-have-spoken).

References

Anderson, P. (2014). Pro-charter schools groups spending huge cash. *The Albany Project.* Retrieved from http://thealbanyproject.com/pro-charter-schools-lobbying-cash/

Bakeman, J. (2014, May 30). Business groups fighting back in support of the Common Core. *Capital.* http://www.capitalnewyork.com/article/albany/2014/05/8546262/business-groups-fighting-back-support-common-core

Bakeman, J. (2015a, February 26). Most NY urban teachers rated highly on student test scores. *Capital.* Retrieved from http://www.capitalnewyork.com/article/albany/2015/02/8563000/most-ny-urban-teachers-rated-highly-student-test-scores

Bakeman, J. (2015b, March 31). An outline of education reform proposals in budget. *Capital.* Retrieved from http://www.capitalnewyork.com/article/albany/2015/03/8565264/outline-education-reform-proposals-budget

Ball, S.J. (2015). Education, governance and the tyranny of numbers. *Journal of Education Policy, 30*(3), 299–301. http://dx.doi.org/10.1080/02680939.2015.1013271

Bellafante, G. (2015, March 24). Exposing hedge fund politics, and getting personal. *The New York Times.* A-24. Retrieved from http://www.nytimes.com/2015/03/29/nyregion/exposing-hedge-fund-politics.html

Blain, G. & Lovett, K. (2015, January 21). Andrew Cuomo unveils big education plan, budget proposal in annual "state of the state" address. *Daily News.* Retrieved from http://www.nydailynews.com/news/politics/cuomo-unveils-big-education-plan-state-state-talk-article-1.2086990

Bryant, E. (2014, June 13). Governor silent on school segregation. *Democrat and Chronicle.* Retrieved from http://www.democratandchronicle.com/story/news/local/columnists/bryant/2014/04/26/bryant-governor-silent-school-segregation/8176951/

Cala, W. (2015, January 22). Letter to parents of children in the Fairport, NY, school district.

Carroll, M. (2015, March 18, 2015). *New York Gov. Cuomo Drops to Lowest Score Ever, Quinnipiac University Poll Finds; Governor Losing School Battle to Teachers' Unions.* Hamden, CT: Quinnipiac University.

Chapman, B. (2014, May 29). City to pay $11G per student in three Success Academy charter schools booted from public space by Mayor de Blasio. *New York Daily News.* Retrieved from http://www.nydailynews.com/new-york/education/city-pay-11g-student-charter-schools-booted-public-space-article-1.1810843

Connor, R. (2015, February 17). Cuomo ties state aid to his education reform agenda. *Hudson Valley News Network.* Retrieved from http://hudsonvalleynewsnetwork.com/2015/02/17/cuomo-ties-state-school-aid-education-reform-agenda/

Craig, S. (2015, March 31). Shopping for yacht? New York budget offers a tax break. *The New York Times,* A22. Retrieved from: http://www.nytimes.com/2015/03/31/nyregion/shopping-for-yacht-new-york-budget-offers-a-tax-break.html

Cuomo, A. W. (2014, March 4). Video and transcript. Gov. Cuomo at charter school rally: Education is about the students, and the students come first. Governor Cuomo website. Retrieved from https://www.governor.ny.gov/news/video-transcript-gov-cuomo-charter-school-rally-education-about-students-and-students-com

Decker, G. (2014, December 18). Cuomo seeks King's "best advice" on crafting aggressive education agenda. *Chalkbeat New York.* Retrieved from http://ny.chalkbeat.org/2014/12/18/cuomo-seeks-kings-best-advice-on-crafting-aggressive-education-agenda/#.VSaYRhfsMkM

Democrats for Education Reform (n.d.). Principles. http://www.dferorg/org/about/principles

Dewitt, K. (2015, January 20). Cuomo outlines infrastructure plans, says he'll take on states "education industry." *WXXI News.* Retrieved from http://wxxinews.org/post/cuomo-outlines-infrastructure-plans-says-hell-take-states-education-industry#.VL6meWlenk4.twitter

Editor. (2015, April 9). Get educated about testing: Students largely forgotten in debate over opting out of Common Core exams. *Democrat and Chronicle,* 13A.

Education Law Center (2015). New York: ELC advocacy for education rights. Education Law Center. Retrieved from http://www.edlawcenter.org/initiatives/new-york-elc-advocacy-for-education-rights.html

Friedman, M. (1995, June 23). "Public Schools: Make Them Private" Cato briefing paper—from *Washington Post.* Briefing Paper No. 23. Retrieved March 16, 2004, from http://www.cato.org/pubs/briefs/bp- 023.html

Friedman. M. & Friedman, R. (1990). *Free to Choose: A Personal Statement.* New York: Houghton Mifflin Harcourt.

Goldberg, J. (2007, June 5). Public schools flunk every course. *Democrat and Chronicle,* 12A.

Goldberg, J. (2008). Liberal fascism: The secret history of the left, from Mussolini to the politics of meaning. New York: Broadway Books.

Gonzalez, J. (2015, April 14). Fed-up parents revolt against state's standardized tests. *New York Daily News.* Retrieved from http://m.nydailynews.com/new-york/education/fed-upparents-revolt-state-standardized-tests-article-1.2185433

Governor's Office. (2015, January 21). *2015 Opportunity Agenda.* Albany, NY: Governor's Office. Retrieved from https://www.governor.ny.gov/news/2015-opportunity-agenda

Haar, Charlene K. (1996, September/October). Special Interests in the Classroom. Fixing America's Schools, American Enterprise Online. *American Enterprise Institute.* Retrieved April 1, 2015, from http://www.unz.org/Pub/AmEnterprise-1996sep-00035?View=PDF<http://www.taemag.com/issues/articleID.16288/article_detail.asp

Haertel, E. H. (2013, March 22). Reliability and validity of inferences about teachers based on student test scores. *Wiliam H. Angoff Memorial Lecture Series*. Princeton, NJ: Education Testing Service.

Harris, E. A. & Fessenden, F. (2015, May 20). "Opt out" becomes anti-test rallying cry in New York State. *New York Times*, A1. Retrieved from www.nytimes.com/2015/05/21/ nyregion/opt-out-movement-against-common-core-testing-grows-in-new-york-state.html

Hursh, D. (2013). Raising the stakes: High-stakes testing and the attack on public education in New York. *Journal of Education Policy*, 28(5), 574–588. doi: 10.1080/026 80939.2012.758829

Johnson, D. C. & Salle, L.M. (2004, November). *Responding to the Attack on Public Education and Teacher Unions: A Commonweal Institute Report*. Menlo Park: CA: Commonweal Institute. Retrieved November 25, 2004, from http://www.commonwealinstitute.org/ IssuesEducation.htm

Joseph, G. (2015, March 19). 9 billionaires are about to remake New York's public school: Here's their story. *The Nation*. Retrieved from http://www.thenation.com/article/20 1881/9-billionaires-are-about-remake-new-yorks-public-schools-heres-their-story

Kaplan, T. & Taylor, K. (2012, January 17). Invoking King, Cuomo and Bloomberg stoke fight on teacher review impasse. *The New York Times*, A17.

Karlin, R. (2015, March 30). Going on the offense, NYSUT's Magee calls for test boycott. *Capital Confidential*. Retrieved from http://blog.timesunion.com/capitol/archives/231 494/going-on-the-offense-nysuts-magee-calls-for-test-boycott/

Kucsera, J. (2014, March 26). New York State's Extreme School Segregation: Inequality, Inaction and a Damaged Future. Los Angeles. *The Civil Rights Project of UCLA*. Retrieved from http://civilrightsproject.ucla.edu/research/k-12-education/integrati on-and-diversity/ny-norflet-report-placeholder

Lovett, K. (2014, October 27). Cuomo will push new teacher evaluations, vows to bust school "monopoly" if elected. *New York Daily News*. Retrieved from http://www. nydailynews.com/news/politics/cuomo-vows-bust-school-monopoly-re-elected-arti cle-1.1989478

Marcou-O'Malley, M. (2014, August). Billions behind: New York State continues to violate students' constitutional rights. *Alliance for Quality Education*. Retrieved from http://www.aqeny.org/wp-content/uploads/2014/08/REPORT-NY-Billions-Behind.pdf

McDermott, M. (2015, March 28). Monroe schools shorted $443M. *Democrat and Chronicle,* A1, A10.

New York City Department of Education. (2015). Charter Schools. New York City Department of Education. Retrieved from http://schools.nyc.gov/community/ planning/charters/Directory

New York City Parents. (2012, December 4). What we talk about when we talk about the Common Core. Retrieved from nycpublicschoolparents.blogspot.com/2012/12/ what-we-talk-about-when-we-talk-about.html

New York State Allies for Public Education. (2015a, January 21). New Yorkers Call FOR an immediate independent investigation of Governor Cuomo for unconstitutional interference in education policy and violations of NY State public officer ethics law. Retrieved from http://www.nysape.org/new-yorkers-call-for-an-immediate-indepen dent-investigation-of-governor-cuomo.html

New York State Allies for Public Education. (2015b, April 23). NY parents have spoken. Now it's time to fix Cuomo's education debacle and establish new leadership for the

Board of Regents. Retrieved from http://www.nysape.org/nysape-pr-ny-parents-have-spoken.html

New York State Department of Education. (2012a, August 13). Guidance on New York State's Annual Professional Performance Review for teachers and principals to implement education law 3012c and the Commissioner's regulations. Retrieved from http://www.engageny.org/wp-content/uploads/2012/05/APPR-Field-Guidance.pdf.

New York State Department of Education. (2012b). New York State teacher and principal evaluation 2012–13 and beyond: Summary of revised APPR provisions. Retrieved from http://www.engageny.org/wp-content/uploads/2012/03/nys-evaluation-plans-guidance-memo-march-2012.pdf (accessed 8 March, 2012).

New York State School Boards Association. (2003, September 16). Title I accountability status updated for March 10, 2003. Retrieved from http://www.nyssba.org/adnews/misc/thenewaccountability-5.htm

New York Times. (2014, September 9). New York State Primary Election Results. Retrieved from http://elections.nytimes.com/2014/results/primaries/new-york-state

New York Times Editorial Board. (2015, September 18). Gov. Cuomo takes on education. *The New York Times*, A-26. Retrieved from http://www.nytimes.com/2015/01/22/opinion/gov-cuomo-takes-on-education.html

Otterman, S. (2011, May 13). Teacher reviews will put more focus on state tests. *The New York Times*, A-17. Retrieved from http://www.nytimes.com/2011/05/14/nyregion/ny-teacher-evaluations-will-emphasize-test-scores-more.html?_r=0

Randolph, E. (2014, June 2). Is Andrew Cuomo liberal? *The New York Times.* Retrieved from http://takingnote.blogs.nytimes.com/2014/06/02/is-andrew-cuomo-liberal/

Ravitch, D. (2012, February 21). No student left untested. *The New York Review of Books.* Retrieved from http://www.nybooks.com/blogs/nyrblog/2012/feb/21/no-student-left-untested/

Ravitch, D. (2014, September 10). The crisis in our schools: Is there a future for public education? Skype presentation at East High School, Rochester, New York.

Ravitch, D. (2015a, March 29). Nearly 100 Superintendents Sign Petition to Save Public Education in NY. Retrieved from http://dianeravitch.net/2015/03/29/nearly-100-superintendents-sign-petition-to-save-public-education-in-ny/

Ravitch, D. (2015b, March 30). Dozens of teacher associations endorse "I refuse" resolutions. Retrieved from http://dianeravitch.net/2015/03/30/dozens-of-ny-teacher-associations-endorse-i-refuse-resolution/

Ravitch, D. (2015c, April 2). Regent Cashin of New York speaks out against high-stakes testing. Retrieved from http://dianeravitch.net/2015/04/02/regent-cashin-of-new-york-speaks-out-against-high-stakes-testing/

Ravitch, D. (2015d, April 11). New York Senate wall of shame and wall of fame. Retrieved from http://dianeravitch.net/2015/04/11/new-york-senate-wall-of-shame-and-wall-of-fame/

Saratogian New York. (2015, January 15). Video with transcript: State of the State. Retrieved from http://www.saratogian.com/general-news/20150121/video-wtranscript-state-of-thestate-2015

Sawchuk, S. (2014, October 9). N.Y. unions sue over Common-Core testing "gag order." *Education Week.* Retrieved from http://blogs.edweek.org/edweek/teacherbeat/2014/10/ny_union_sues_over_common-core.html

Schneider, M. K. (2014). *A Chronicle of Echoes: Who's Who in the Implosion of American Public Education.* Charlotte, NC: Information Age Publishing.

Seller, C. (2014, December 30). Cuomo vetoes own bill. *Times Union*. Retrieved from http://www.timesunion.com/local/article/Cuomo-vetoes-own-bill-5986558.php

Stossel, J. (2013, October 2). Let's call our public schools what they really are—"government" schools. The Fox News. Retrieved from http://www.foxnews.com/opinion/2013/10/02/let-call-our-public-schools-what-really-are-government-schools/

Strauss, V. (2011, December 7). Are half of New York's teachers really "not effective"? *The Washington Post*. Retrieved December 7, 2011, from http://www.washington post.com/blogs/answer-sheet/post/are-half-of-new-yorks-teachers-really-not-effec tive/2011/12/05/gIQAhDXyaO_blog.html

Strauss. V. (2012, April 17). What the U.S. can't learn from Finland in education reform. *The Washington Post*. Retrieved from http://www.washingtonpost.com/blogs/answer-sheet/post/what-the-us-cant-learn-from-finland-about-ed-reform/2012/04/16/gIQAGIvVMT_blog.html

Strauss, V. (2015, January 1). Teacher evaluation: Going from bad to worse? The Washington Post. Retrieved from http://www.washingtonpost.com/blogs/answer-sheet/wp/2015/01/01/teacher-evaluation-going-from-bad-to-worse/

Taylor, K. (2014, December 29). Cuomo vetoes bill that would have protected teachers from low ratings. *The New York Times*. Retrieved from http://www.nytimes.com/2014/12/30/nyregion/cuomo-in-reversal-vetoes-bill-that-would-have-pro tected-teachers-from-low-ratings.html?hpw&rref=education&action=click&pgtype=Homepage&module=well-region&region=bottom-well&WT.nav=bottom-well

Taylor, K. (2015a, January 20). Cuomo's education agenda sets battle lines with teachers' unions. *The New York Times*, A-17. Retrieved from http://www.nytimes.com/2015/01/21/nyregion/cuomos-education-agenda-sets-battle-lines-with-teachers-unions.html

Taylor, K. (2015). Cuomo fights rating system in which few teachers are bad. *The New York Times*, A1. Retrieved from http://www.nytimes.com/2015/03/23/nyregion/cuomo-fights-rating-system-in-which-few-teachers-are-bad.html

Teachout, Z. & Khan, M. (2014, December 2). Corruption in New York: Hedge Funds and the Takeover of New York's Schools. *The Washington Park Project*. Retrieved from http://www.aqeny.org/wp-content/uploads/2014/12/Hedge-Fund-White-Paper-Teachout-Final-Formatted-2.pdf

Teachout, Z. & Wu, T. (2014). Teachout Wu Education. Retrieved from http://www.teachoutwu.com/education

U.S. Department of Education. (n.d.). *Race to the Top*. Washington, DC: Author. Retrieved from http://www2.ed.gov/programs/racetothetop/index.html

Winerip, M. (2012, January 22). In Race to the Top, the dirty work is left to those on the bottom. *The New York Times*, A15. Retrieved from http://www.nytimes.com/2012/01/23/education/in-obamas-race-to-the-top-work-and-expense-lie-with-states.html.

WNBZ News (2014). Teachers picket Whiteface Lodge/Camp Philos education retreat. *WNBZ News*. Retrieved from http://www.wnbz.com/2014/05/teachers-picket-whiteface-lodge-camp-philos-education-retreat/

4

THE GATES FOUNDATION, PEARSON, AND ARNE DUNCAN

In the previous chapters, I have argued that educational policy making has shifted from the local and state levels to the state, federal, national, and international. Two exemplars of international organizations are The Bill and Melinda Gates Foundation and Pearson. The Gates Foundation is the largest philanthropic organization in the world, headed by the wealthiest person in the world. Pearson is the largest education corporation in the world. Arne Duncan has significantly expanded the power of the federal secretary of education by holding states to the requirement under NCLB that states have a 100% passing rate on the standardized tests or, as part of obtaining a waiver or gaining funding under Race to the Top, submit to even more federal requirements.

In this chapter, I show how Gates, Duncan, and Pearson share five assumptions about reform based on the neoliberal imaginary, whether it is about education or, in the case of the Gates Foundation, also about global health and food security. In addition, because of the shift from government to governance and the shift from hierarchy to heterarchy, philanthropic organizations and corporations can more easily collaborate on and benefit from their political connections and projects. Consequently, I suggest, Gates has the greatest individual impact on education policy, Pearson the most significant corporate influence while Pearson Education is headed by Sir Michael Barber, heads change, so I will refer to it as Pearson, as if it were a person, which, of course, the U.S. Supreme Court says it is in Citizens United v. Federal Elections Commission (2010) and in Burwell v. Hobby Lobby (2014), and Duncan the most political.

The five neoliberal assumptions they share are as follows:

First, they promote privatization and markets to solve what are social and political problems. For the Obama administration and the Gates Foundation, the solution to improving education is privatization, as RTTT requires states to raise the limit on the number of charter schools permitted. Gates promotes KIPP (Knowledge is Power Program) charter schools as the ideal schools and funds hedge fund managers for events such as the recent "Bonds and Blackboards" (Gonzalez, 2015) in New York City where they can explore the multiple ways in which they can profit off of charter and parochial schools.

Second, Gates, Pearson, and Duncan propose solutions to societal problems that assume that the political, economic, and social context do not matter. Whether considering global health, food, or education, they assume that the reforms can succeed without examining and remedying the economic and structural inequalities. In the same way that other neoliberals claim that "poverty does not matter," Gates, Pearson, and Duncan ignore the underlying structures that cause the social inequalities.

For example, the Gates Foundation is often lauded for its efforts to improve global health. However, Anne-Emanuelle Birn (2005), professor of International Development Studies and Canadian Chair of International Health at the University of Toronto, faults the foundation's Grand Initiatives in health for their over-reliance on technology and for ignoring the more complicated but necessary political and economic issues. She states that the Foundation's Grand Challenges in health:

> [S]hare an assumption that scientific and technical aspects of health improvement can be separated from political, social, and economic aspects. Indeed, the Grand Challenges initiative has made this division explicit by excluding the problems of poverty, access to health interventions, and delivery systems.
>
> (Birn, 2005, p. 516)

Birn argues that without examining social, political, and economic inequalities, efforts to improve global health are likely to fail. She states that "redistribution measures . . . play a key role in the successful implementation of medical, public health, educational, and household measures" (p. 514). Without decreasing poverty, Birn adds, global health is unlikely to improve. "Relative poverty—as reflective of hierarchies of access to material, social, and political power—demonstrates a clear gradient effect, whereby each step down the ladder is associated with worse health" (p. 515).

Birn highlights a third characteristic of their reform proposals: their reliance on technological solutions. The federal RTTT initiative requires that the Common Core standardized tests be administered on computers. Gates and Pearson are collaborating in New York on the Common Core assessments and curriculum. Both hope that the CCSS will make it possible to deliver curriculum using Microsoft software, computers, and tablets to all the students throughout the nation.

By focusing on technological rather than political solutions, Gates' global health and agriculture initiatives may worsen rather than improve conditions.

For example, producing more food will not necessarily increase food security. In 2010, India produced more food per capita than previously, but because of the focus on exports rather than local consumption and the corporate monopoly over bioengineered seeds rather than those saved by farmers, more people are going hungry than before (Null, 2009; Shiva, 2005). Similarly, hunger in Africa has increased because the World Bank's and International Monetary Fund's economic policies undermined the ability of local farmers to grow food for local consumption. During the 1960s, "Africa," writes Bello:

> [W]as not just self-sufficient in food but was actually a net food exporter, averaging 1.3 million tons in food exports a year between 1966 and 1970. Today, the continent imports 25 percent of its food, with almost every country being a net importer.
>
> (Bello, 2009, p. 68)

The reform proposals of Gates, Pearson, and Duncan share a fourth characteristic: they promote private solutions to public problems. Almost 60 years ago, critical sociologist C. Wright Mills (1959) noted that our personal problems, whether they include hunger, poverty, or social alienation, must be connected to the larger structural forces that affect our lives. We need to understand our personal troubles as public issues. However, by promoting markets, choice, and technological solutions, Gates, Duncan, and Pearson undermine public efforts to engage in collectively solving our problems.

Fifth, Block and Somers (2014) prefer the term "market fundamentalism" to neoliberalism because, as they describe, proponents of unregulated free markets have an unreasonable faith or quasi-religious certainty that markets can exist without regulation. Likewise, Gates, Pearson, and Duncan express an unsubstantiated faith that their proposals will result in improving education and reduce the incidences of diseases and hunger.

Moreover, Bill Gates seems to admit that his reform initiatives, which have included developing small schools and improving teacher quality but now focus on the Common Core standards, curriculum, and tests, are based not on research but faith and consequently may or may not work. In a 2013 speech he admitted that "it would be great if our education stuff worked, but that we won't know for probably a decade" (Strauss, 2015a). Bill Gates imposes his view of education reform on the United States—as the corporate reform initiative spreads to other countries, what Pasi Sahlberg (2011) calls the GERM (Global Education Reform Movement)—without evidence that it will work. In contrast, as Sahlberg describes, Finland, over a span of several decades, used research primarily from the United States to reform their schools. They placed their faith not in markets but on the ability of educators to create and teach innovative curriculum and pedagogy based on the national standards. In addition, rather than the endless high-stakes testing that students in New York face, Finnish students have only one test during their senior year as they apply to university. They have also worked to create a society in which there is minimal economic inequality and poverty, and education from preschool through university is free.

Therefore, while the corporate reforms have failed to improve education and now, at least in New York, are causing great damage, the only thing of which we can be sure is that some people have grown very wealthy and powerful. In the rest of this chapter, I will turn to specific analyses of Gates, Pearson, and the Obama administration to provide further evidence for my claims so far.

The Bill and Melinda Gates Foundation

Surprisingly, there have been few in-depth analyses of the Gates Foundation, with Kovacs (2011) as the most notable collection of analyses. I suggest that there are at least two reasons for the lack of critiques. First, his earlier projects focusing on small schools and better preparing teachers had a limited impact on the field of education and were not well known outside of the education profession. Second, progressive educators, as Klonsky and Klonsky (2008) described regarding the small schools movement in Chicago, may have hoped to use Gates' wealth for progressive purposes. However, as Gates ended the small schools project, turned to blaming teachers for the shortcomings of urban schools, and took up the CCSS as his primary initiative, his political and philosophical assumptions were exposed. Moreover, in his financial and strategic support for the CCSS, he has had the greatest impact on education policy and practices in the United States not only in terms of what is instantiated—high-stakes testing and corporate curriculum— but what is marginalized and extinguished—assessments and curriculum locally developed by educators in response to the needs and interests of the students in particular schools.

In education, we can see many of the same themes that are evident regarding health and agriculture: an oversimplification of the problem that ignores the larger social, economic, and political context; a reliance on technological remedies, including standardized tests; and concentrating decision-making power on either the corporate or institutional leaders while marginalizing teachers, parents, students, and other community members.

In this section, I begin by describing Gates' initial involvement in funding small learning communities and then in developing small schools and continue by addressing how these efforts, in part because they were top-down efforts that excluded teachers, parents, and students, often failed to improve student achievement and in some cases were abandoned. Consequently, Bill Gates shifted his strategy from reforming schools to creating new ones with decision-making power concentrated in the hands of administrators. In his January 2009 Annual Report (2009a) and February 2009 talk at the annual Technology, Entertainment, Design Conference (TED), Bill Gates (2009b) extolled the virtues of the KIPP charter schools, suggesting them as the solution to increasing educational achievement.

While, according to Gates, teachers should have little input on educational goals or school organization, teachers are almost entirely responsible for student achievement. Differences in student achievement, he claims, result not from differences in resources provided schools nor social and economic inequalities such as lack of health care nor adequate housing but because of differences in teacher quality. Students who do well do so, he argues, because they have better teachers.

Furthermore, he asserts that superior teachers are created not through teacher education programs or professional development but because they use students' test scores for the feedback necessary to improve. He states that testing is the only objective measurement of our students and that the scores inform teachers how to improve. His entire approach to education concentrates on test scores.

The Gates Foundation entered into school reform efforts in 2001 when, in response to the student shootings in Columbine, Colorado, Congress appropriated $48 million for creating smaller learning communities (SLCs) in larger high schools. The advantage of SLCs, Congress argued, were that they would allow teachers to better know students and that schools would, therefore, be safer. Congress allotted $125 million for this initiative, to which the Gates Foundation added $1.5 billion.

In Chicago, the funding enabled groups of teachers, led by William Ayers, to develop the Small Schools Workshop in which teachers, administrators, and parents developed small schools. The principles that guided their work were taken from successful small schools, such as Deborah Meier's Central Park East in New York City, that included teachers working together to design schools in which teachers team teach, develop curriculum that builds on students' interests, and collaboratively assess students' learning. The key to the schools' success was that the teachers could respond to the needs and interests of the students and the students could come to feel that they are a valuable part of a learning community.

However, as Klonsky and Klonsky (2008) describe, the Gates Foundation's approach to developing SLCs undermined the structural advantages of SLCs. The Gates Foundation views teachers as a group to be controlled rather than consulted. In Chicago, a Foundation representative, in response to a question of whether teachers would be part of a Gates-funded board that governed the public schools, declared that teachers could not be part of the board because that would be a conflict of interest, "like having the workers running the factory" (Klonsky & Klonsky, 2008, p. 13).

Eventually, the Gates' top-down approach to school reform met with disaster, which led to the Gates Foundation deciding to no longer support the conversion of large high schools into small learning communities. Instead, the director of the Gates school reform projects argued for closing "a thousand schools" (Klonsky & Klonsky, 2008, p. 134), and they turned their attention to starting new schools from scratch as either charter schools or corporate-run schools. For example, in Chicago, the Gates Foundation became a principal supporter of Renaissance 2010, which included closing 100 schools and reopening two-thirds of them as either charter schools or schools run by outside agencies. The Foundation contributed $100 million to the Chicago reform effort.

In his recent annual report, Bill Gates reflected on the changes in their reform approach:

> Nine years ago, the foundation decided to invest in helping to create better high schools, and we have made over $2 billion in grants. The goal was to give schools extra money for a period of time to make changes in the way they were organized (including reducing their size), in how the teachers worked, and in the curriculum. The hope was that after a few years they would operate at the same cost per students as before, but they would have become more effective.
>
> Many of the small schools that we invested in did not improve students' achievement in any significant way. . . . We had less success trying to change an existing school than helping to create a new school.
>
> (Gates, 2009a, p. 11)

Subsequently, as indicated by their involvement in the recent meeting in New York of hedge-fund managers seeking to make a profit from privatizing schools (Gonzalez, 2015), the Gates Foundation now advocates establishing charter schools characterized by top-down administration and standardized curriculum and tests. In recent reports and lectures, Gates argued that the difference between students succeeding or failing is in the quality of their teachers. While there is some truth in the claim that the teacher quality makes a difference, Gates concludes that the differences from school to school in student success has to do almost entirely with the quality of teachers, therefore ignoring differences in resources provided either in the school or at home including educational resources, a commitment of local government to enriching educational programs outside of school, a time and place to study, and access to free or affordable medical care. In his talk at TED, Gates concludes:

> [T]he more we looked at it, the more we realized that having great teachers was the very key thing. And we hooked up with some people studying how much variation is there between teachers, between, say, the top quartile—the very best—and the bottom quartile. How much variation is there within a school or between schools? And the answer is that these variations are absolutely unbelievable. A top quartile teacher will increase the performance of their class—based on test scores—by over 10 percent in a single year.
>
> (Gates, 2009b, p. 1)

Gates' thinking is more than a little circular. He assumes that high tests scores prove that the teacher is of high quality, a characteristic that remains undefined, and then claims that if we only had high-quality teachers, students' tests scores would increase, so "if the entire U.S., for two years, had top quartile teachers, the entire difference between us and Asia would go away." Gates, B. (2009b February 11). Of course, that means somehow quadrupling the number of high-quality teachers when, in states like New York, the reforms associated with implementing Gates' CCSS is decimating enrollments in teacher education programs.

Furthermore, in response to the question of how to create high-quality teachers, he argues that advanced degrees, such as a master's degree in education, make no difference, nor do years of teaching. Rather, he says the best predictor of whether a teacher will be a good teacher is previous performance. Such thinking leaves unanswered how a teacher becomes good to begin with.

However, later in his TED address, he suggests we use the model of KIPP schools to understand how to create good teachers. KIPP schools, of which there are currently 162 in the 20 states plus the District of Columbia serving some 59,000 students, are characterized by a longer school day, including school on some Saturdays, a standardized curriculum emphasizing behavioral modification techniques and repetition, and teachers being on call 24/7. Parents need to sign a contract pledging that their child will comply with requirements and disciplinary measures. As we note below, what little data we have about the schools indicates that there is a high attrition rate for both students and teachers (KIPP, n.d.).

Gates argues that in KIPP schools, teachers improve because they look at the data and conclude that their teaching is the cause of increased learning. However, as we know from statewide standardized tests, tests often inflate student achievement and are not a reliable indicator of student achievement from one year to the next (Hursh, 2008, 2013). Further, higher test scores by themselves do not tell teachers what, exactly, about their teaching is leading to the increased learning. In fact, the Common Core exams only give a score from 1 to 4 and no other information.

Moreover, the KIPP school data on their own schools is suspect. For example, while students graduating from KIPP schools may have, on average, higher test scores than other students in the district in which the school is located, the schools are characterized by having a high attrition rate. In a study undertaken at four San Francisco area KIPP schools, 60% of the entering fifth graders had left by the end of the eighth grade (Robelen, 2008, p. 10). If, on average, those students who are either pushed out or drop out of KIPP schools are the lower achieving students, as they are likely to be, then the remaining students are likely to be more capable and perform better on tests. As is true for charter schools in general, high test scores can be achieved by pushing out students who are likely to lower the scores or not graduate.

Also, like charter schools in general, KIPP schools have a high teacher turnover rate. In the San Francisco study, the "annual turnover rate for faculty ranged from 18% to 49% from 2003–04 to 2007–08" (Robelen, 2008, p. 10). As such,

KIPP schools resist accountability and marginalize parents, students, and teachers. Parents and students are forced to sign a contract stating what they will do in order to stay in the school. Teachers are perceived as workers who should have no say in shaping curriculum and pedagogy. In New York, where charter schools over a minimum size are required by law to allow teachers to unionize, KIPP schools are resisting the teachers' efforts (Medina, 2009).

Gates and Common Core State Standards

Common Core State Standards would not exist if it were not for Bill Gates. Consequently, because of the political resistance to, especially, the Common Core standardized exams, the educational activities of Bill Gates and the Gates Foundation have become increasingly visible to the public. At first, the supporters of the CCSS sold the standards as a result of a grassroots voluntary initiative to raise and unify standards across the 50 states. However, over time a more complicated story emerged, one that deserves a full, in-depth study, the best of which exists in Mercedes Schneider's book, *A Chronicle of Echoes: Who's Who in the Implosion of American Education* (2014a) and in her blog at https://deutsch29.wordpress.com/.

As Layton (2014) reports, the CCSS were dying for lack of support until Gene Wilhoit, the former Council of Chief State School Officers (CCSSO), and David Coleman, the CCSS "lead architect" and now president of the College Board, approached Gates in the summer of 2008 for support. According to Layton, Gates exceeded Wilhoit and Coleman's hopes by taking CCSS on as his personal project. How much Gates has given to support the CCSS may not be calculable. We do know that Gates responded, according to Ravitch (2013), with $200 million to support to CCSS but has since added billions. Hassard (2014) reports that Gates:

> [H]as provided $2.3 billion in support of the Common Core, with more than 1800 grants to organizations running from teachers unions to state departments of education to political groups like the National Governor's Association [that] have pushed the Common Core into 45 states, with little transparency and next to no public review.
>
> (P. 2)

Schneider has calculated that Gates gave the National Governors Association $23.6 million to "work with state policy makers on the implementation of the CCSS . . . as well as rethinking state policies on teacher effectiveness." From 2009 to the present, the four organizations responsible for CCSS—the National Governors Association, Common Core State Standards Organization, Achieve, and Student Achievement Partners—have taken $147.9 million from Bill Gates. Gates has also given millions to the major education organizations: National Education Association ($4 million); American Federation of Teachers ($5.4 million); and Education Trust, which publishes *Education Week* ($2 million).

Gates has granted 16 universities a total of $17.6 million for CCSS imple-mentation. I list the universities and the amounts they received because some of the figures are significant, leading one to conclude that the universities might significantly impact the debate over the CCSS. The universities and the amounts received are: DePaul $248,343; George Washington $259,895; Harvard $557,168; MIT $3,004,132; Michigan State $650,000; NYU $40,282; Purdue $1,453,832; UCLA $942,527; Stanford $2,292,500; Arizona $3,416,901; Flor-ida $250,000; Kentucky $1,000,000; Michigan $1,999,999; Missouri $249,826; and Washington $610,819.

Schneider (2013) writes that not one grant was used for piloting CCSS in order to see how well it worked prior to implementation. One grant—to the State University of New York (SUNY) for $600,000—uses the word "pilot," not to pilot CCSS but to produce "professional development." SUNY's Chancellor, Nancy Zimpher, after receiving the funding, announced that she will head the university group Higher Education for Higher Standards that supports the CCSS, suggesting that the funding is to support universities in promoting the CCSS.

In fact, during first week of Common Core state testing in April 2015, Zim-pher weighed in against the parent opt out movement, releasing a statement that parents should not opt their children out of the standardized tests because "for too long our education system has failed to track students' progress toward college and career readiness.... Parents, educators and policymakers have an obligation to use standardized assessments to shine a light on how best to sup-port students" (Harding, 2015). Ravitch (2015) quickly responded to Zimpher's statement, saying that "nothing" that Zimpher wrote "is true. The information provided by the tests is worthless. It is a score. It offers no information about how to help students improve. It gives a score and a ranking compared to others in the state."

As I mentioned in an earlier chapter, Gates has also provided funding to the New York State Education Department to implement the Common Core State Standards. The Gates Foundation provided $3 million over three years to John King, the previous commissioner of education, so that he could hire 27 secret advisors, with expertise primarily in testing and who are paid more than $200,000 each. Funding for these advisors came from Gates and several other philanthropic foundations, including the Helmsley Charity and the Tisch Foundation, both of which also gave $3 million. The Tisch Foundation is funded by the chancellor, to whom the commissioner reports (Odato, 2013), thereby ensuring that the com-missioner carried out the chancellor's wishes.

In addition to funding secret advisors, the Bill and Melinda Gates Foundation and the Helmsley Charity also fund High Achievement New York, a nonprofit coalition composed almost entirely of business groups (for a list, see Schneider, 2014b) that launched a $500,000 phone and digital advertising campaign to pro-mote the CCSS in New York (Bakeman, 2014). High Achievement New York has, not surprisingly, pushed back against the opt out movement by using many of the same arguments of the corporate reformers. They claim that the teachers are only protecting their own interests while the business groups are about all children learning.

"The calls coming from the New York State Teachers Union for parents to opt their kids out of this week's state exams are nothing more than political self-preservation. Their arguments are based on what is best for the union, not what is best for our children and their future." (Briccetti & Sigmund, 2015, p. 1) Instead, as stated by Steve Sigmund, the executive director of High Achievement New York and coauthor Bricetti, the assessments "are the best way to make sure every child had basic reading and math skills" (Briccetti & Sigmund, 2015, p. 1). They reiterate the myth that the CCSS were developed in partnership with teachers and principals, when the reality is that teachers and principals were only brought in in the end to ratify what had already been done. They also repeat Chancellor Tisch's comparison of the Common Core standardized tests as similar to a "doctor's checkup." Finally, like Cuomo and others, they describe teachers as a special interest, stating that: "The tests are not a political issue— even if *special interests* use these assessments as a wedge to improve their standing in political negotiations."

Comparing, as Tisch, High Achievement, and others have, the Common Core tests to a doctor's visit fails on several grounds. First, doctors vary the physical depending on the patient, asking different questions and assessing different biological systems based on the age, gender, race, and previous history of the patient. Second, the patient receives not just a single number as an assessment ("Your health is a 3.") but multiple measures, including blood pressure, weight, and results from a variety of blood tests. Third, physicals do not last for ten hours over six days, as New York's Common Core tests do (Strauss, 2015b).

Finally, not only has Gates' funding provided overwhelming support for the CCSS in New York but Gates has a national impact that I have only briefly indicated by his invited dinner speeches to the United States Senate. However, Gates previously has funded and worked closely with the Duncan administration, essentially supplying Duncan's senior appointees. Schneider (2014c) reveals that what Duncan's advisors have in common is not experience in traditional public schools but in promoting privatization. She writes that:

> They have been appointed to carry out the work of condemning and supplanting the traditional K12 American classroom with profitable "ventures" and disposable teachers by relentlessly testing the traditional classroom, collecting unprecedented amounts of data on it; labeling it a failure; replacing it with under-regulated, philanthropic-padded, market-driven "reform" that is also supposed to channel students to serve the market, and all the while adding the USDOE padding to their corporate-favoring resumes and advancing their own careers in the process.
>
> (Schneider, 2014c P. 3)

Schneider's research demonstrates the strong networking between the Obama administration and the Gates Foundation regarding support for privatization and the Common Core State Standards, which states were strongly urged to adopt if they hoped to receive RTTT funding. As Schnieder states:

> New York State was roped into declaring CCSS as a condition of its RTTT funding. . . . Arne Duncan wants all to believe that RTTT does not require CCSS; however, the RTTT application did require "common standards" and "common assessments," and the National Governors Association (NGA) and the Council of State School Officers (CCSSO) just happened to make the a CCSS MOU (memorandum of understanding) available for governors and state superintendents to sign in spring 2009—and Duncan allowed the CCSS MOU as proof of a state's intent to commit itself to . . . "consortia-developed standards" for which he agreed to fund associated "consortia-developed assessments."
>
> (Schneider, 2014b P. 4)

Gates and Duncan are able to coordinate their efforts because personnel who are committed to privatization, profits, technology and other corporate reforms move between the Gates Foundation and the secretary of education's office. The two current Gates' connected personnel are Jim Shelton, the deputy secretary of education, and Ted Mitchell, undersecretary of education. Both have connections to the Bill Gates-funded NewSchools Venture, which invests in charter schools and technology and where Mitchell was CEO, for which he was paid $735,000 over five years. Mitchell has close ties with Pearson and the privatization movement, serving on over a dozen boards promoting privatizing schools. In an interview for *Forbes* when he was with the NewSchools Venture Fund, Mitchell highlighted KIPP and Aspire as the best schools and Teach for America as the best teacher education program.

As described, Gates also aims to reform teacher education around the idea that learning to teach primarily requires assessing student progress through standardized test scores and using those scores to adapt one's practice. Among the unknown number of teaching organizations in New York that he funds is Educators 4 Excellence (E4E). E4E is a New York-based organization funded by the Gates Foundation and other corporate reform organizations such as Education Reform Now, mentioned above regarding Camp Philos, which promotes charter schools, ending tenure, and "Seniority-based layoffs" (Pelto, 2015). E4E is composed primarily of current and past Teach for America teachers. Gates provided initial funding of $160,000 to E4E in 2010, which was funneled through Stand for Children, a group supporting privatization and charter schools, and then another $3 million in 2013.

In this chapter and book, I have not tried to research and reveal Bill Gates' national and global impact but, instead, to indicate some of his efforts in New York. Bill Gates uses his fortune to fund the corporate education reform focusing on the Common Core standards, curriculum, and assessment and on privatizing education through charter schools. In addition, as evidenced by his funding of organizations such as the NewSchools Venture Fund, he is interested in developing projects that will create profits for investors. He engages in these reforms, acknowledging that he does not know how successful they will be nor considering, as in health and agriculture, whether they undermine more promising approaches to solving what are at base social and economic problems.

I have also tried to indicate how the shift in governance to heterarchical networks facilitates the ability of wealthy individuals and organizations to impact policy, often without public awareness. In writing about Gates' role in creating the CCSS, High Achievement New York, Education Reform Now E4E, it should be clear how these organizations are interconnected and funded by similar organizations, including the Gates and Walton Foundations and the Helmsley Charity. They together use their amassed power to control policy and marginalize families and teachers.

Pearson in the United States and New York

Pearson is the world's largest education corporation that seeks to not only dominate education globally but also to dominate all aspects of education, as Ball observes:

> [A]cross all three educational 'message systems'—pedagogy, curriculum, and assessment and joining these up, globally, across a range of media, within its product and business growth plan. Its publishing and curriculum and assessment work contributes to define what cultural knowledge is most worthwhile and these products have invested them with particular conceptions of educational organization and process.
>
> (Ball, 2012, p. 127)

Pearson, more than Gates and Duncan, exemplifies how, in seeking profit, corporations aim to colonize educators' expertise, commodify it, and sell it back to educational institutions, thereby marginalizing educators. Harvey (2005) refers to this process as "accumulation by dispossession," which is "the redistribution of public or commonly held assets and resources, through privatization and financialization" (Ball, 2012, p. 33). Moreover, as we have seen in New York, teachers are given curriculum developed by and bought from Pearson to prepare the students for the Pearson-developed tests. Consequently, the public in general and educators in particular are excluded from the process.

While Gates influences education policy by funding thousands of organizations favoring privatization, standardized testing, and Common Core curriculum, Pearson dominates education through creating and administering most of the standardized tests and publishing most of the textbooks. Among the textbook and publishing companies that Pearson owns are Adobe, Scott Foresman, Penguin,

Longman, Wharton, Harcourt, Puffin, Prentice Hall, Allyn & Bacon, and Random House. Pearson also creates and administers most of the standardized exams in the United States, including the National Assessment of Educational Progress, the Stanford Achievement Test, the Miller Analogy Test, and the Graduate Equivalency Diploma. They also have a major contract with Gates to develop and administer the Partnership for Assessment of Readiness for College and Careers (PARCC, 2015), which claims to assess whether students are on track to be college and career ready. PARCC is currently in 15 states.

In New York and in most states, Pearson creates, administers, and grades the CC exams in language arts and math. The contract in New York is worth $32.1 million over five years. Pearson also has the state and national account for the edTPA, which assesses teacher education students for certification.

Globally, Pearson now holds the contract from the Organization for Economic and Cooperative Development (OECD) to create and administer the PISA (Programme for International Student Assessment) exams. PISA is the most well-known international exam that many countries perseverate over.

One key for Pearson is that all of these exams are delivered on computers. However, the technology sometimes fails. On this day, the first day of Common Core testing nationally, Ravitch reports via her blog that a Pearson server crashed in Colorado while tens of thousands of students were taking online assessments in social studies and science. Computers also crashed in Minnesota, Tennessee, Nevada, Montana, and North Dakota, and that is only what has been reported so far.

One indication that Pearson may be expanding too quickly and lacks qualified personnel was the recent Multi-Subject certification exam administered by Pearson for New York State. Students in the Rochester area who registered for the exam and had received confirmation as to the day, time, and place of the exam arrived at the venue only to find the doors to the building locked. Upon calling NYSED, the students were quizzed regarding whether it was a mistake on their part. Once NYSED was satisfied that the students' description of the problem was accurate, the students were told to contact Pearson. Upon reaching Pearson, they were informed that there was nothing they could do, nor could they refund the students, but that the students could initiate a claim. A week later, Pearson contacted the students to inform them that they could reregister for the test for "no additional fee." At no time did Pearson apologize or explain why test takers were instructed to show up for a test at a site with no one to administer it (M. Anthony, personal communication with the author, April 25, 2015).

The Obama Administration: We Have Seen the Future and the Future Is Corporatized

As I have described, Arne Duncan and the Obama administration have been deeply disappointing (Hursh, 2015). They have increased the corporatization and privatization of education as they have, through RTTT, increased the high-stakes nature of standardized testing by linking test scores to teachers' evaluations, required states to adopt curriculum that prepares students to be college and career ready, effectively limited schools to adopting the Common Core State Standards and exams, and required states to remove or significantly raise limits on the number of charter schools if states wanted to win funding under RTTT competition or a waiver from the NCLB requirements.

As Diane Ravitch summarized, under RTTT states are required:

> [T]o adopt "college and career-readiness standards," which most states understood as the Common Core State Standards (CCSS) that were funded mainly by the Gates Foundation and promoted by the Obama administration. They had to agree to test students to measure progress toward meeting the goals of college and career readiness; these were the tests funded by the Obama administration to assess the Common Core standards. They had to agree to submit their standards and assessments to the U.S. Department of Education for review. They had to agree to evaluate teachers and principals using student test scores as a significant part of their evaluation. They had to agree to establish a system of recognizing schools as "reward," "focus," and "priority" schools, which were the lowest performing. They had to develop a plan to establish measurable objectives for all their schools.
>
> (Ravitch, 2013, p. 282)

Furthermore, Duncan and his staff have been, like most corporate reformers, deaf to the concerns of parents, students, and teachers. When parents objected to the high failure rates on the first iteration of the Common Core exams, Duncan dismissed them as out of touch with their children and schools. However, as Schneider (2013) recounts, Duncan has not been interested in parents discussing curriculum, assessment, or teachers. Instead, parents are to be Friedman's (Friedman & Friedman, 1990) optimal choosers in a market, choosing good schools for their children. In 2010, Duncan spoke to the first annual "Mom Congress," telling parents that:

> Parents can serve in at least one of three roles: *Partners in learning, advocates and advisors who push for better schools, and decision-makers who choose the best educational options for their children.*
>
> When parents demand change and better options for their children, they become the real accountability backstop for the educational system. *Parents have more choices today than ever before, from virtual schools to charters to career academies.* And our schools need empowered parents.
>
> We need parents to speak out and drive change in chronically-underperforming schools where children receive an inferior education.

> With parental support, those struggling schools need to be turned around
> now—not tomorrow, because children get only one chance at an education.
> (Mercedes in Schneider 2013, p. 1)

For Duncan, parents are not to question the reforms, the curriculum, or the tests. Rather, they are to choose the "best education options for their children," including choosing from "virtual schools, charters, and career academies" (Duncan, 2010). They are to support the administration's policies.

No wonder, then, that Duncan blasted parents who complained the results on the Common Core exams did not reflect their child's abilities, which, as I have described, barely more than 30% of New York's students passed. Duncan responded by saying he found it "fascinating" that some of the opposition to the Common Core exams were, "White suburban mom who—all of a sudden—their child isn't as brilliant as they thought they were" and their school not as good as they thought. (Mercedes in Schneider 2013, p. 1)

Given that the passing rate on the exams was determined before the test was administered shows that the parents were correct in objecting that the tests were invalid representations of what students knew. Parents knew that the "fix was in."

Rick Hess (2012), a conservative educator who has supported much of the reform movement, argued that the low passing rate on the Common Core exams was intended to set off an uprising of suburban parents against the public schools and to demand charter schools and vouchers (funding for private schools). However, parents in the United States generally approve of their local schools and most knew that the results were not accurate reflections of their children or schools (Bushaw & Calderon, 2014 a and b).

The Obama administration has carried out the neoliberal agenda as they have worked to privatize education through charter schools and funding private organizations and, in almost all cases, Pearson and Microsoft to create and deliver the curriculum and tests. Increasingly, what teachers know and can do is not only not valued but is seen as threatening to an education system in which what and how students are to learn and how they are to be assessed is determined at corporate headquarters. Those in power retain their power through their wealth and connections. The leaders of the corporate reform movement are unelected and unaccountable, composing both an oligarchy and plutocracy; they aim to monopolize educational discourses, structures, and processes.

In the next chapter, I describe what we might do to reclaim education as an activity that is guided by students and teachers.

References

Bakeman, J. (2014, May 30). Business groups fighting back in support of the Common Core. *Capital*. Retrieved from http://www.capitalnewyork.com/article/albany/2014/05/8546262/business-groups-fighting-back-support-common-core

Ball, S. J. (2012). *Global Education, Inc.: New Policy Networks and the Neoliberal Imaginary.* New York: Routledge.

Bello, W. (2009). *Food Wars.* New York: Verso.

Birn, A-E. (2005). Gate's grandest challenge: Transcending technology as public health ideology. *The Lancet, 366,* pp. 514–519.

Block, F. & Somers, M. (2014). *The Power of Market Fundamentalism.* Cambridge, MA: Harvard University Press.

Briccetti, H.C. & Sigmund, S. (2015, April 23). View tests as a checkup on education. *High Achievement New York.* Retrieved from http://www.highachievementny.org/latest_news

Bushaw, W. J. & Calderon, V. J. (2014a, September). The 46th annual PDK Gallup poll of the public's attitudes toward the public schools: Part One. *Phi Delta Kappan, 96*(1), 9–20.

Bushaw, W. J. & Calderon, V. J. (2014b, October). The 46th annual PDK Gallup poll of the public's attitudes toward the public schools. Part Two. *Phi Delta Kappan, 96*(2). 48–59.

Duncan, A. (2010, May 3). Looking in the mirror: Final remarks of Secretary Arne Duncan to the Mom Congress. *U.S. Department of Education.* Retrieved from http://www2.ed.gov/news/speeches/2010/05/05032010.html

Friedman. M. & Friedman, R. (1990). *Free to Choose: A Personal Statement.* New York: Houghton Mifflin Harcourt.

Gates, B. (2009a, January). 2009 Annual letter from Bill Gates. Retrieved from http://www.gatesfoundation.org/who-we-are/resources-and-media/annual-letters-list/annual-letter-2009

Gates, B. (2009b, February 11). Bill Gates' talk on mosquitoes, malaria and education—transcribed. TED Blog. Retrieved from http://blog.ted.com/bill_gates_talk/

Gonzalez, J. (2015, March 11). Hedge fund executives give 'til it hurts to politicians, especially Cuomo, to get more chart schools. *New York Daily News.* Retrieved from http://www.nydailynews.com/new-york/education/hedge-fund-execs-money-charter-schools-pay-article-1.2145001

Harding, R. (2015, April 14). SUNY chancellor on upcoming state tests: "If kids opt out, we risk them being left behind" *Auburnpub.* Retrieved from http://auburnpub.com/blogs/eye_on_ny/suny-chancellor-on-upcoming-state-tests-if-kids-opt-out/article_1d449340-e21b-11e4-a9ad-a37110a2d391.htm

Harvey, D. (2005). *A Brief History of Neoliberalism.* Oxford: Oxford University Press.

Hassard, J. (2014, March 15). Why Bill Gates defends the Common Core. *The Art of Teaching Science.* Retrieved from http://www.artofteachingscience.org/why-bill-gates-defends-the-common-core/

Hess, R. (2012, November 30). The Common Core Kool-Aid. *Education Week.* Retrieved from http://blogs.edweek.org/edweek/rick_hess_straight_up/2012/11/the_common_core_kool-aid.html

Hursh, D. (2008). *High-Stakes Testing and the Decline of Teaching and Learning.* Lanham, MD: Rowman & Littlefield.

Hursh, D. (2013). Raising the stakes: High-stakes testing and the attack on public education in New York. *Journal of Education Policy, 28*(5), 574–588. doi: 10.1080/02680939.2012.758829

Hursh, D. (2015). Even more of the same: How free market education dominates education. *The Phenomenon of Obama and the Agenda for Education: Can Hope Audaciously Trump Neoliberalism?* Charlotte, NC: Information Age Press.

KIPP. (n.d.). Frequently asked questions. Retrieved from http://www.kipp.org/faq

Klonsky, S. & Klonsky, M. (2008). *Small Schools: Public School Reform Meets the Ownership Society*. New York: Routledge.

Kovacs, P.E. (Ed.). 2011. *The Gates Foundation and the Future of U.S. "Public" Schools*. New York: Routledge.

Layton, L. (2014, June 7). How Bill Gates pulled off the swift Common Core revolution. *The Washington Post*. Retrieved from http://www.washingtonpost.com/politics/how-bill-gates-pulled-off-the-swift-common-core-revolution/2014/06/07/a830e32e-ec34-11e3-9f5c-9075d5508f0a_story.html

Medina, J. (2009, February 6). Teachers say union faces resistance from Brooklyn charter school. *New York Times*, A15. Retrieved from http://www.nytimes.com/2009/02/07/education/07kipp.html?_r=0

Mills. C.W. (1959). *The Sociological Imagination*. Oxford: Oxford University Press.

Null, G. (2009, January 3). Globalization and poverty: An interview with Dr. Vandana Shiva. *Share the world's resources: Sustainable economics to end world poverty*. Accessed: http://www.stwr.org/food-security-agriculture/globalization-and-poverty-an-interview-with-dr-vandana-shiva.html

Odato, J.M. (2013, November 25). Education reform backed by the wealthy. *Times Union*. Retrieved from http://www.timesunion.com/local/article/Wealth-backs-reform-team-5006670.php

Partnership for Assessment of Readiness for College and Careers (2015). About PARCC. Retrieved from http://www.parconline.org/about-parcc

Pelto, J. (2015, April 22). Educators 4 Excellence—Because teachers NEED their own "education reform" front group. Retrieved from http://jonathanpelto.com/2015/04/22/educators-4-excellence-because-teachers-need-their-own-education-reform-front-group/

Ravitch, D. (2013). *Reign of Error: The Hoax of the Privatization Movement and the Danger to America's Public Schools*. New York: Knopf.

Ravitch, D. (2015, April 14). The utter uselessness of the Common Core tests: Opt out. Retrieved from http://dianeravitch.net/2015/04/14/the-useful-information-teachers-get-from-state-tests/

Robelen, E.W. (2008, September 28). KIPP study finds high student attrition amid big learning gain. *Education Week*, *18*(5), 10.

Sahlberg, P. (2011). *Finnish Lessons: What Can the World Learn from Educational Change in Finland?* New York: Teachers College Press.

Schneider, M. K. (2013, November 17). Some kids "aren't brilliant"? This Duncan blunder is bigger than it first appears. https://deutsch29.wordpress.com/2013/11/17/some-kids-arent-brilliant-this-duncan-blunder-is-bigger-than-it-first-appears/

Schneider, M. K. (2014a). *A Chronicle of Echoes: Who's Who in the Implosion of American Public Education*. Charlotte, NC: Information Age Publishing.

Schneider, M. K. (2014b, October 28). High Achievement NY: Common Core must work because we don't want to face Arne. Retrieved from https://deutsch29.wordpress.com/2014/10/28/high-achievement-ny-common-core-must-work-because-we-dont-want-to-face-arne/

Schneider, M. K. (2014c, November 23). Obama's USDOE: Appointed to Privatize. Period. Retrieved from https://deutsch29.wordpress.com/2014/11/23/obamas-usdoe-appointed-to-privatize-period/

Shiva, V. (2005). *Earth Democracy: Justice, Sustainability, and Peace*. Cambridge, MA: South End Press.

Strauss, V. (2015a, April 3). What the 'thoughtless' N.Y. government just did to teachers. *The Washington Post.* Retrieved from http://www.washingtonpost.com/blogs/answer-sheet/wp/2015/04/03/what-the-thoughtless-n-y-government-just-did-to-teachers/

Strauss, V. (2015b, April 16). Why the debate between Diane Ravitch and Merryl Tisch was remarkable. *The Washington Post.* Retrieved from http://www.washingtonpost.com/blogs/answer-sheet/wp/2015/04/16/why-the-debate-between-diane-ravitch-and-merryl-tisch-was-remarkable/

5

MANUFACTURED AND REAL CRISES

Rethinking Education and Capitalism

We face both a manufactured and real crisis. We face a manufactured crisis as corporate reformers manipulate test scores and misrepresent the data to have us believe that our public schools are failing so that public schools can be privatized. For Andrew Cuomo, portraying the public schools as failing provides a rationale for breaking "the public school monopoly" and, like Wisconsin's Governor Scott Walker (Davey & Smith, 2015), for attacking teachers and teachers' unions. For Arne Duncan and his newly hired consultant, New York's recently resigned commissioner of education John King, the hope is that middle-class families, whom Arne calls the "suburban moms," would rise up and demand school privatization through charter schools or vouchers for their children (Strauss, 2013).

By depicting the public schools as failing, the corporate reformers, as Ravitch states, aim to distract our attention from several real crises Ravitch, D. (2013). These crises include, as I have described in previous chapters:

- Corporate reformers have hijacked the discourse of reform, positioning themselves as the "real reformers" while describing educators as defenders of the status quo. They have gained control over how education policy is made while marginalizing educators, parents, students, and community members. In New York, hedge fund managers, charter school CEOs, Governor Cuomo, and Arne Duncan and his assistants promote policies that benefit themselves and their allies.
- While the corporate reformers portray themselves as acting in the interests of the students, they have used their power to advance their own power and wealth. They have passed laws that benefit investors in charter schools and real estate. Furthermore, the push for standardized testing and a uniform curriculum has already benefited Microsoft and Pearson as they develop

standardized exams and curriculum available on Microsoft technology. Bill Gates, with his $14 billion in Microsoft stock, and Pearson, as the largest producer of standardized exams, reap huge profits from supporting the Common Core State Standards.

- The corporate reformers claim that using standardized exams to hold students, teachers, and schools accountable will, on their own, increase learning, reduce the achievement gap, and, consequently, decrease social and economic inequality. At the same time, they ignore data showing that neither the achievement gap nor inequality is declining. The data show that our society is becoming more unequal, with more families and children living in poverty (Sommeiller & Price, 2015). In addition, our schools are becoming increasingly unequal and segregated. Moreover, the schools that serve the most challenged students—those with disabilities, English language learners, or who live in poverty—are most likely to focus on test prep curriculum rather than curriculum that meets the students' needs. Standardized tests harm the students most in need of a challenging, culturally appropriate curriculum.

- Given the complex social, economic, and environmental challenges, it is crucial that schools give students the opportunity to learn to think holistically and solve problems that do not have an agreed upon answer. However, standardized tests, by narrowing the curriculum and limiting learning to a narrow range of skills, undermines students' abilities to respond to environmental and social problems, such as climate change, toxins in our environment, and inequality. In fact, some educators (Bigelow & Swinehart, 2014) have argued that it is unethical to not use schooling to prepare students to tackle complicated political, environmental, and ethical issues.

- Neoliberals undermine democratic deliberation in two ways: by claiming that all decisions should be made through market mechanisms and, at the same time, ignoring that many important decisions are made not through market mechanisms but instead covertly by the powerful and the wealthy. For example, as I described, the campaign to adopt the Common Core State Standards was largely directed and funded by the Gates Foundation with little public conversation. Further, Arne Duncan and his senior advisors come from organizations that have promoted and benefited from privatization and standardized testing.

- Lastly, we are constrained not only by the neoliberal imaginary of market fundamentalism, but also traditional economic theory that limits our ability to conceptualize the world differently.

Consequently, in this last chapter I want to argue that we need to respond to the above crises by undertaking three simultaneous, complementary projects that acknowledge the three interrelated social conflicts I described in the first chapter. We need to defend public education as worth public funding and as an area in which everyone has input, rather than only those who are wealthy or have political connections.

- We need to counter the dominant social imaginary of neoliberalism and the faith in market fundamentalism with a social imaginary that understands that government does and must have a role in our society, that democratic deliberation is part of the political process, and that economic policies should incorporate values beyond economic growth and profit. In particular, our new social imaginary needs to transform our relationship to nature to create a more sustainable planet (Sachs, 2011).
- We need to push back against those promoting the neoliberal agenda that has contributed to the increasing inequality between the wealthiest 1% and the other 99%. Income has stagnated for the bottom 99% while the top 1% becomes wealthier. The most recent statistics show that between 1979 and 2012, the income for the top 1% increased by 180.9% and the other 99% by a mere 2.6%. For all but the very rich, income has increased slightly more than one-tenth of 1% per year. Currently, the average income for the top 1% is 30 times greater than the bottom 99% (Sommeiller & Price, 2015). Furthermore, these figures would be more lopsided if we compared wealth—real estate and other assets—and not only income (Lowrey, 2013). Consequently, children in the United States are increasingly likely to live in poverty, and more than half do so.
- The neoliberal agenda to cut governmental funding is reflected not only in the cuts to elementary and secondary education but also higher education and societal infrastructure, such as transportation and utilities. In New York, funding for the state universities has been continually reduced, requiring universities to raise tuition in an attempt to make up the deficit. Wisconsin's Governor Walker has proposed a $300 million cut in funding to the University of Wisconsin (Bosman, 2015). Because much of the university's expenses are fixed, such as upkeep on buildings and grounds, the area most likely to be effected is the number of faculty and their salaries.
- The neoliberal agenda is promoted and implemented by those in political office such as Governors Cuomo and Scott Walker; organizations such as the American Legislative Exchange Council (ALEC); and wealthy funders of such groups, such as the Koch brothers. The Koch brothers fund numerous neoliberal and neoconservative organizations, including Americans for Prosperity and the American Energy Alliance (Robbins, 2014). They also have announced that they plan to spend $889 million on favored politicians in the upcoming 2016 campaign, which is a greater amount than either the Democrats or Republicans as political parties have spent in past elections (Confessore, 2015). The Koch brothers wield more power than any other individual or political party. Restoring public funding for both public schools and public governance requires political action on many fronts.

- Education policy is increasingly determined not at the local and state levels, where, until recently, most decisions were made, but at the federal and national levels. Furthermore, high-stakes tests are used as the lynchpin to, as Ball (1994) writes, steer policy "from a distance" (p. 54). Therefore, we need to develop democratic processes that place educators, parents, and students in the center of decision making. Such changes will require more than protesting the neoliberal agenda; it will also necessitate developing new social structures.

Therefore, in this concluding chapter, I will begin by describing why neoliberalism/market fundamentalism must be replaced by a social democratic imaginary. I will remind us that the neoliberal claim that markets must be free of governmental regulation is either naïve or intentionally misleading. In fact, what neoliberals have succeeded in doing is reregulating markets to suit their own purposes (Wacquant, 2010). Furthermore, market fundamentalism fails to consider anything that cannot be measured monetarily, thus failing to take into account our effects on nature. However, responding to environmental crises, such as climate change, requires incorporating nonmonetary values.

We need, therefore, to both rethink the state and the economy. The historian and social critic Tony Judt, in *Ill Fares the Land* (2010), wrote, "in short, the practical need for strong state and intervention in government is beyond dispute. But no one is 're-thinking' the state" (p. 8). He adds, "the choice will no longer be between the state and the market, but between two sorts of states. It is thus incumbent upon us to reconceive the role of government if we do not, others will" (p. 9).

Therefore, I am not interested in returning to the social democracy of the 1960s. The rise of the network society (Castells, 1996), the end of hierarchy and emergence of heterarchy, and the shift from government to governance is permanent (Suspitsyna, 2010). Instead, I suggest that we need to make public how decision making occurs. If there are to be charter schools funded by public money, they should become public institutions, which in New York, they are not.

Rolling Back the Neoliberal Imaginary and Creating a New Social Democratic Imaginary

We need to roll back the neoliberal reforms because they advance the neoliberal social imaginary, undermine democracy, and increase economic and social inequality. In response, I suggest that we need to create new social imaginaries that take into account more than narrow financial calculations and must include our relationship with one another and with nature. Further, we need to create a society where individuals and families are provided with, as Franklin Roosevelt proposed over 70 years ago with his second Bill of Rights, "the right to a remunerative job ... to a decent home ... adequate medical care ... [and] a good education" (Sunstein, 2004, ix).

In addition, not only neoliberalism but also traditional economics do not generally account for the effects that economic activities have on nature. Environmental costs such as carbon in the atmosphere, plastic and other toxic pollutants in our water, and poisons in our food are not only missing from economic calculations but described as "externalities" that become the responsibility of the public to suffer and to remedy, while corporations continue to make a profit. For example, energy companies continue to profit while putting more carbon into the atmosphere, and the public pays as it cleans up from the damage caused by the more powerful storms caused by global warming. Therefore, we need to expose the ways in which neoliberals have created a manufactured crisis in education by misrepresenting the state of education and, instead, respond to the real crises of economic inequality and poverty, the degradation of our environment, climate change, environmental destruction, and species extinction (Klein, 2014; Kolbert, 2014; Zimmer, 2015).

We need to counter the faith-based economics of market fundamentalists who, like Hayek, assume that markets are much more efficient at allocating resources and goods than individuals. In fact, Hayek goes as far as to describe the market as having knowledge that individuals could not possibly possess; as Mirowski (2013) writes, Hayek believed that "the market really does know better than any one of us what is good for ourselves and society" (p. 54). Furthermore, because markets are purportedly the most efficient way to make societal decisions, any resulting economic and political inequality is not only necessary, but also beneficial. Again, Mirowski (2013), writing on Hayek, observes that inequality is "a necessary functional characteristic of their ideal market system" (p. 79). But in contrast to some other forms of economic liberalism, for neoliberals, any economic, social or political attempts to alter the outcomes of markets are necessarily counterproductive, for these would violate the "natural order" of the market. As Block and Somers (2014) observe, such "market fundamentalism" rests upon the idea of social naturalism, which is "a way of viewing the world built on the assumption that the laws governing natural phenomenon also govern human society" (p. 102).

Consequently, both proponents and critics of neoliberalism often state that neoliberalism aims to reduce or eliminate government, such as Grover Norquist of Americans for Tax Freedom, who blatantly declared that he "doesn't want to abolish government. I simply want to reduce it to the size where I can drag it into the bathroom and drown it in the bathtub" (cited in Klein, 2007, p. 446). However, scholars also note that certain neoliberals embrace the notion that government has a key role in *reregulating*, not deregulating, the economy in favor of corporations. We see this in how governments organize markets and society for a variety of "human activities, including the private provision of core public goods" (Wacquant, 2010, p. 213). In New York State, for example, charter schools would not exist if the state government did not (i) create the legal framework for establishing and operating charter schools, (ii) grant charter school operators public funding and the right to free or reduced-cost space in public schools buildings, and (iii) provide tax deductions and other benefits to investors.

Thus, we have no choice but to interfere in the creation and organization of markets. The question, therefore, is not whether we should or should not, but in what ways should we organize markets so that they serve societal needs as we live on this finite planet (Zincey, 2012).

Rethinking Networks, Heterarchy, and Public Education

To state a platitude, globalization and technology have transformed society and there is no going back. How and who has input on education policy has changed. In this last part, I want to reassert the public in public education.

For example, if we are to have privately managed, publicly funded charter schools, we should require that they permit anyone to visit, have public board meetings, and make public their fiscal accounting. Instead, we learn that the charter schools in New York are holding $282.3 million in the bank in reserve. While traditional public schools are limited to holding 4% of the budget in reserve, the 200 charters in New York have 25.3% of their annual budgets in reserve (NYSUT, 2015). Moreover procharter groups, such as the Families for Excellent Schools, spent $2.9 million on lobbying efforts in the two months before the recent election (Anderson, 2014).

Likewise, who has influence in Albany or Washington, D.C. should be made apparent. Knowing how the Common Core was developed should not be a secret, nor should that the Gates Foundation funded 1,800 organizations to support the CCSS. Nor should it take several years to reveal that New York's commissioner of education has 12 advisors funded by neoliberal foundations supporting high-stakes testing (Odato, 2013). Nor that hedge fund managers and (Campanile, 2014) groups supporting charter schools are spending millions on lobbying the governor and the legislature. Moreover, decisions cannot only be made, as they are now, by those who have power or wealth. However, those who have power are not likely to surrender it, and it will, therefore, need to be contested.

As described earlier, educators and parents in New York have pushed back against the Common Core standards, curriculum, and standardized tests. Thousands have shown up at forums conducted by the commissioner of education or state legislative committees. In March 2015, almost 100 forums were organized across the state by parents and teachers in response to Cuomo's education proposals to base 50% of a teacher's evaluation on students' scores on the state Common Core exams. The governor also proposed requirements making tenure almost impossible to achieve. Cuomo's proposals, as I described in depth in chapter 3, were passed in the legislature with only slight modifications.

Parents and teachers, who have voiced over the last several years their displeasure with the direction the corporate reforms have taken, have realized that neither the legislature, regents, commissioner, chancellor, nor governor are listening. Consequently, many parents have decided that the only response left is to opt their children out of the standardized exams. In 2014, about 60,000 children statewide opted out of the exams. This year, the total opting out for the first week of the English language arts exam is close to 200,000. The number opting out of the second week's math exams is about another 5% higher, but not all the districts have reported the number of opt outs for the language arts exam and they are just coming in for the math exams. Final numbers by district, which will be public by the time this is published, are available at "2015 Refusal Policy Counts" (NYSAPE, 2015b).

In Monroe County, where the city of Rochester is located, 16 districts reported the percentage of third through eighth grade students opting out. The Rochester City School District and two suburban districts have not reported. Of those reporting, the highest opt out rate was 67.1%, and the lowest was 19.6%. Adding up the total numbers, 33.2 % of the students did not take the exam on the first day it was given. Many think that more students will opt out on subsequent days.

The Rochester City School District is not only not providing the figures; a district administrator sent a letter to school principals asking them to provide the names of any teachers who encourage parents or students to opt out and to report teachers who were absent on testing day.

The letter received a quick response from the president of the Rochester Teachers Union, Adam Urbanski. Urbanski's described the letter sent to principals as:

> [A] blatant attempt at intimidation and an infringement on teachers' rights and academic freedom. . . . As well they should, teachers should feel a moral obligation to speak up when they witness harm being done to their students. I applaud all parents who choose to refuse to subject their children to these meaningless and bad tests. . . . Today we have filed a Class Action Grievance against the District for taking disciplinary actions against individual teachers. . . . We will continue to defend the rights of teachers to speak out against harmful educational practices and to advocate for the best interest of their students.
>
> (Ravitch, 2015)

Statewide, the opt out numbers are also high, particularly in the suburbs of Long Island, east of New York City. Some districts reported an opt out rate of 60 to 65%. As reported by Gonzalez,

> [T]he entire structure of high-stakes testing in New York crumbled Tuesday, as tens of thousands of fed-up public school parents rebelled against Albany's fixation with standardized tests and refused to allow their children to take

the English Language Arts State exam. . . . But this was not provoked by any politician or the teachers unions, as some want you to believe. . . . Tens of thousands of parents got tired of being ignored by the people in Albany. So one fine day in April, they simply said, "no more."

(Gonzalez, 2015 p. 2)

Those who are opting out hope that the high percentage of students opting out will make invalid evaluating teachers and schools based on their test scores invalid, and, therefore, the regents, who are officially but not in practice the body that makes decisions about education policy for the state, would cancel the tests. That parents were able to organize other parents in their school to opt out at such a high rate, often as they are threatened by school and district administrators to that opting out will result in cuts to the school's funding, is remarkable.

However, whether the whole testing regime will crumble is still an open question. Those who have not listened to the parents in the past and have economic reasons to continue the testing—who want to portray the public schools as failing so that privatization can proceed apace—are not likely to give in easily.

The initial response from the New York State Education Department (NYSED) is that the tests will go ahead. "We are confident that the department will be able to generate a representative sample of students who took the test, generate valid scores for anyone who took the test, and calculate valid state-provided growth scores to be used in teacher evaluations" (Murphy, 2015).

But one wonders how fair it is to evaluate an elementary teacher based on the test scores of one- to two-thirds of her students. In addition, NYSED admits the situation is further complicated because some students showed up for the first day of testing and not for the second; those students will receive a score for the exam of 1, the lowest of four possible scores.

Furthermore, Arne Duncan has raised the possibility of the federal government intervening to punish the states. Duncan has stated that it is up to the states to ensure that districts have no fewer than 95% of students taking the tests; if states do not ensure that, then "we have an obligation to step in" (Wall, 2015).

What will happen is unclear. Parents are saying that the standardized testing regime reflects a system in which educators and parents are not trusted to evaluate what is occurring in their own schools, and teachers and parents want their schools back from the governor, the chancellor, Gates, Pearson, and Duncan. At least some of the mainstream media have noted that the mass refusal indicated the failure of the governor's and Tisch's reform program. The Editorial Board of the Journal News declared that "The stunning success of the test refusal movement in New York is a vote of no confidence in our state educational leadership" and called for Chancellor Tisch to resign (NYSAPE, 2015a).

Two members of the New York Alliance for Public Schools echo the concerns I have raised regarding the influence of the Gates Foundation and other so-called philanthropic organizations and the privatization of public services. Anna Shah,

Dutchess County public school parent and the founder of Schools of Thought in Hudson Valley, NY, states that:

> On Chancellor Tisch's watch, the work of the State Education Department has been outsourced to a privately funded 'Regents Fellows' think tank. It is not surprising that the reforms put forth by this think tank advance the agenda of the wealthy 'yacht set' and corporate-linked groups that fund the Regent Fellows: The Robin Hood Foundation, Gates Foundation, and even Chancellor Tisch herself. When you replace a public service with a private organization that advances corporate agendas, New Yorkers know that is corruption.
>
> (NYSAPE, 2015a)

Fred Smith, who is described as a testing specialist and retired NYC public schools administrative analyst, blasts the standardized tests and the chancellor for their lack of transparency, accountability, and the way in which the scores are manipulated.

> Instead of transparency and disclosure of complete and timely test data that would open the quality of the ELA and math exams to independent review, Tisch has ruled over an unaccountable testing program that flies at near-zero visibility—in a fog of flawed field testing procedures, age-inappropriate poorly written items, the covert removal of test questions after they have been scored, arbitrarily drawn cut off scores, and the misapplication of the results to reach unsupportable conclusions about students, teachers, and schools.
>
> (NYSAPE, 2015a)

NYSAPE has issued an initial list of six demands: Chancellor Tisch's resignation, reduce the amount of testing in grades three through eight, "conduct an independent review of the college and career ready standards to ensure the standards are research based and appropriate," "adhere to a public and transparent process for selecting a new NYS Commissioner of Education," pass new legislation "that decouples student test scores and restores local board of education control over teacher evaluations," and "pass legislation that requires parental consent to share any identifiable student data beyond school district administrators" (NYSAPE, 2015a).

Nonetheless, while parents and teachers have managed to accomplish an almost impossible goal—convincing on average one-third of parents to opt their children out of the standardized exams in an effort to accomplish the goals described above—nothing has changed yet. Moreover, the billionaire hedge fund managers, Gates, Pearson, and the groups spending billions of dollars on the legislature in New York are not about to give up and will impact not only state but also federal education policy.

Democratic candidate for president Hillary Rodham Clinton faces the dilemma of whether she will side with the parents and educators who are pushing the demands summarized above or side with the wealthy hedge fund managers who support the Cuomo agenda of privatization, high-stakes testing, and denigrating teachers (Haberman, 2015). John Petry, a hedge fund manager and cofounder of the Harlem Success Academy charter school, makes clear the connection between hedge fund managers, campaign funding, and privatization, when he states that "donors want to hear where she stands" (Haberman, M. 2015, March 24 p. A1).

Resurrecting Positive Conceptions of Political: Rethinking Education and Society

We cannot rely on faith-based economics or education but must work to develop a society that responds to the problem of how we live on a finite planet that has limited resources and is transformed for better and worse by our actions. This requires that we learn how to engage one another in solving our collective problems. As we work to rethink and remake schools as public community centers where everyone becomes central to creating a more democratic, sustainable, and equal world, we will not only be creating a better educational process but also a better society.

To accomplish these goals, Block and Somers (2014) suggest that we need to rethink our conception of the political, a word often used pejoratively to mean a process abused by those in positions of power. Instead, Block and Sommers (2014) suggest we need to (re)build those social institutions and processes that help solve our collective problems. They advocate an approach, rooted in scholarship, where communities learn from one another past, present, and future and:

> [A]nalyze the varied means by which people cooperate to sustain the kinds of institutions, allocations, and social practices that support collective livelihood. From this perspective, understanding how to best meet the needs of livelihood requires anthropological and historical analysis of actual social practices rather than abstract assumptions and economic axioms.
>
> (Block & Sommers, 2014, p. 226)

Trust and Community

From the beginning, standardized tests scores have been manipulated to portray the public schools as either failing or, because of the introduction of standardized curriculum, as improving, but not improving by so much as to undermine demands that the manufactured educational crisis can only be solved by privatizing schools themselves as charter schools, or by privatizing teaching, curriculum, and assessment through the Common Core State Standards, curriculum, and exams.

As evidenced by Cuomo's continuing attack on teachers as not caring about students and on unions as only caring about protecting their paychecks, the scores have been used to undermine trust in teachers. Rochester's local media state that parents are opting out of the Common Core exams because they are dupes of the teachers' union (Editor, 2015). Duncan belittles "suburban moms" because they object—correctly—that the Common Core test results do not reflect the quality of teaching and learning in their local schools (Strauss, 2013).

However, attacking teachers and removing them from making educational decisions, belittling parents as pawns of teachers, and imposing top-down mandates will only serve to destroy public education. In response, I have called throughout this book for creating a social democracy focused not on the individual but on creating a society based on equality and the common good. Two key components of that society are trust and community.

While Cuomo's attack on public schools and their teachers will increase the funding he receives from hedge fund managers for his election campaigns, he has severely damaged the trust necessary for viable communities and strong schools. In fact, his actions, I fear, are destroying communities and the public schools.

The lack of trust and community exemplified by the corporate education reform policy in the United States is exactly the opposite of what we need. Both trust and community are required as "all collective undertakings require trust" (Judt 2010, p. 63), adding, "the more equal a society, the easier it is to trust" (Judt 2010, p. 66).

The Finnish educator Pasi Sahlberg compares the United States and Finland in an article titled *What the U.S Can't Learn from Finland* (Strauss, 2012). He laments that the United States is not prepared to make the societal changes required to reach the educational achievement level of Finland. These changes include, but are not limited to, providing equal funding to schools regardless of their neighborhood, providing universal health care to children, and providing free education from preschool to university.

As difficult as those changes are, even more difficult, given the last several decades of corporate reforms, is developing trust and community. Sahlberg states, "in Finland, there is a strong sense of trust in schools and teachers to carry out these responsibilities. There is no external inspection of school or standardized testing of all pupils in Finland" (p. 1). Sahlberg continues:

> In the United States, education is mostly viewed as a private effort leading to individual good. The performances of individual students and teachers are therefore in the center of the ongoing school reform debate. By contrast, in Finland, education is viewed primarily as a public effort serving a public purpose. As a consequence, education reforms in Finland are judged more in terms of how equitable the system is for different learners.
>
> (Strauss, 2012, p. 1)

Sahlberg points out that achieving strong educational results requires social equality. Sahlberg cites the Organization for Economic and Cooperative Development report (2012), stating that "The highest-performing education systems across the OECD countries are those that combine quality with equity" (Strauss. V. 2012, April 17 p. 9).

Saving the public schools will require instilling in society a new social imaginary, one that focuses on everyone's welfare and truly does not leave children, families, and neighborhoods behind. It will require rethinking governance, so that everyone is encouraged to take part rather than only those who can pay the $1,000 price of admission, as at Camp Philos. It will require developing networks that include, rather than exclude, and make possible public decisions. It will require, where appropriate, moving decision making back down to the local levels. It will require, as Pizzigatti reminds us in *The Rich Don't Always Win: The Forgotten Triumph Over Plutocracy That Created the American Middle Class* (2012), a concerted political movement against the rich and the powerful. Lastly, it will require retaking our schools from the privateers and making them democratic communities.

References

Anderson, P. (2014). Pro-charter schools groups spending huge cash. *The Albany Project*. Retrieved from http://thealbanyproject.com/pro-charter-schools-lobbying-cash/

Ball, S.J. (1994). *Education Reform: A Critical and Post-Structural Approach*. Buckingham, England: Open University Press.

Bigelow, B. & Swinehart, T. (2014). *A People's Curriculum for the Earth: Teaching Climate Change and the Environmental Crisis*. Milwaukee, WI: Rethinking Schools.

Block, F. & Somers, M. (2014). *The Power of Market Fundamentalism*. Cambridge, MA: Harvard University Press.

Bosman, J. (2015, February 16). 2016 ambitions seen in Walker's push for university cuts in Wisconsin. *The New York Times*. Retrieved from http://www.nytimes.com/2015/02/17/us/politics/scott-walker-university-wisconsin.html?_r=0

Campanile, C. (2014, October 29). Charter Advocates, Teachers Union Are State's Biggest Lobbying Spenders. *New York Post*. Retrieved from http://nypost.com/2014/10/29/charter-advocates-teachers-union-arestates-biggest-lobbying-spenders/

Castells, M. (1996). *The Rise of the Network Society*. Malden, MA: Blackwell.

Confessore, N. (2015, January 26). Koch brothers' budget of $889 million is on par with both parties' spending. *The New York Times*, A1. Retrieved from http://www.nytimes.com/2015/01/27/us/politics/kochs-plan-to-spend-900-million-on-2016-campaign.html

Davey, M. & Smith, M. (2015, February 26). Scott Walker is set to deliver new blow to labor in Wisconsin. *The New York Times*, A14. Retrieved from http://www.nytimes.com/2015/02/26/us/politics/walker-is-set-to-deliver-new-blow-to-labor-and-bolster-credentials.html

Editor. (2015, April 9). Get educated about testing: Students largely forgotten in debate over opting out of Common Core exams. *Democrat and Chronicle*, 13A.

Gonzalez, J. (2015, April 14). Fed-up parents revolt against state's standardized tests. *New York Daily News*. Retrieved from http://m.nydailynews.com/new-york/education/fed-up-parents-revolt-state-standardized-tests-article-1.2185433

Haberman, M. (2015, March 24). Hillary Clinton caught between dueling forces in education: Teachers and wealthy donors. *The New York Times*. Retrieved from http://www.nytimes.com/2015/03/25/us/politics/hillary-clinton-caught-between-dueling-forces-on-education-teachers-and-wealthy-donors.html

Judt, T. (2010). *Ill Fares the Land*. New York: Penguin Books.

Klein, N. (2007). *The Shock Doctrine: The Rise of Disaster Capitalism*. New York: Metropolitan Books.

Klein, N. (2014). *This Changes Everything: Capitalism and the Climate*. New York: Simon & Schuster.

Kolbert, E. (2014). *The Sixth Extinction: An Unnatural History*. New York: Henry Holt and Company.

Lowrey, A. (2013, April 28). Wealth gap among races has widened since recession. *The New York Times*, B1.

Mirowski, P. 2013. *Never Let a Serious Crisis Go to Waste: How Neoliberalism Survived the Financial Meltdown*. New York: Verso Press.

Murphy, J. (2015, April 15). State officials: Test results will still be used. *Democrat and Chronicle*. Retrieved from http://www.democratandchronicle.com/story/news/2015/04/15/rochester-opt-wednesday/25817459/

New York State Allies for Public Education. (2015a, April 23). NY parents have spoken. Now it's time to fix Cuomo's education debacle and establish new leadership for the Board of Regents. Retrieved from http://www.nysape.org/nysape-pr-ny-parents-have-spoken.html

New York State Allies for Public Education. (2015b, May 1). Test refusal totals. Retrieved from http://www.nysape.com.

NYSUT (2015, February 2). Analysis: New York charter schools flush with cash. New York State United Teachers, p1 http://www.nysut.org/news/2015/february/nysut-analysis-shows-ny-charter-schools-flush-with-cash

Odato, J.M. (2013, November 25). Education reform backed by the wealthy. *Times Union*. Retrieved from http://www.timesunion.com/local/article/Wealth-backs-reform-team-5006670.php

Pizzigatti, S. (2012). *The Rich Don't Always Win: The Forgotten Triumph Over Plutocracy That Created the American Middle Class*. New York: Seven Stories Press.

Ravitch, D. (2015). Adam Urbanski defends teachers' freedom of speech. Retrieved from http://dianeravitch.net/2015/04/14/adam-urbanski-defends-teachers-freedom-of-speech/

Robbins, D. (2014, August 27). Myths and facts about the Koch Brothers. *Media Matters*. Retrieved from http://mediamatters.org/research/2014/08/27/myths-and-facts-about-the-koch-brothers/200570

Sachs, J. (2011). *The Price of Civilization: Reawakening American Virtue and Prosperity*. New York: Random House.

Sommeiller, E. & Price, M. (2015, January 26). The increasingly unequal states of America: Income inequality by state, 1917 to 2012. *Economic Policy Institute*. Retrieved from http://www.epi.org/publication/income-inequality-by-state-1917-to-2012/

Strauss. V. (2012, April 17). What the U.S. can't learn from Finland in education reform. *The Washington Post*. Retrieved from http://www.washingtonpost.com/blogs/answer-sheet/post/what-the-us-cant-learn-from-finland-about-ed-reform/2012/04/16/gIQAGIvVMT_blog.html

Strauss, V. (2013, November 16). Arne Duncan: 'White suburban moms' upset that Common Core shows their kids aren't 'brilliant.' *The Washington Post*. Retrieved from http://www.washingtonpost.com/blogs/answer-sheet/wp/2013/11/16/arne-duncan-white-suburban-moms-upset-that-common-core-shows-their-kids-arent-brilliant/

Sunstein, C.R. (2004). *The Second Bill of Rights: FDR's Unfinished Revolution and Why We Need It More Than Ever*. New York: Basic Books.

Suspitsyna, T. (2010). Accountability in American education as a rhetoric and a technology of governmentality. *Journal of Education Policy, 25*(5), 567–586.

Wacquant, L. (2010). Crafting the neoliberal state: Workfare, prisonfare, and social insecu-
rity. *Sociological Forum, 25*(2), 197–220.

Wall, P. (2015, April 21). As opt-out numbers grow, Arne Duncan says feds may have to
step in. *Chalkbeat*. Retrieved from http://ny.chalkbeat.org/2015/04/21/as-opt-out-num
bers-grow-arne-duncan-says-feds-may-have-to-step-in/#.VTqG_RfsMkP

Zimmer, C. (2015, January 15). Ocean life faces mass extinction, broad study says. *The New
York Times,* A1. Retrieved from http://www.nytimes.com/2015/01/16/science/earth/
study-raises-alarm-for-health-of-ocean-life.html

Zincey, E. (2012). *The Other Road to Serfdom and the Path to Sustainable Democracy*. Hanover,
NH: University Press of New England.

INDEX